77 GARDENING QUESTIONS ANSWERED

77 Gardening Questions Answered

For your edible garden

ROHANNE YOUNG, BSC. GRAD DIP. MASTERS IN ENVIRONMENT

The Delectable Garden

Contents

1	OVERVIEW AND PURPOSE	1
2	HOW TO GET STARTED	3
3	PLANNING AND PREPARING	9
4	SOILS AND SUCCESS	13
5	PLANTING YOUR VEGETABLE GARDEN	23
6	WHAT CAN YOU GROW IN YOUR ENVIRONMENT	33
7	ABOUT WATERING AND FERTILISING	39
8	COMPOSTING TO REDUCE WASTE	49
9	WEEDS AND OTHER PLANTS YOU DON'T WANT	59
10	GOOD BUGS AND BAD BUGS	65
11	VISITORS AND GATECRASHERS	82
12	WAYS TO GROW FOOD WITHOUT CHEMICALS	86
13	TIPS TO ENSURE YOUR PLANTS THRIVE	96
14	ABOUT THE AUTHOR	103

Chapter 1

OVERVIEW AND PURPOSE

WELCOME

Fresh vegetables

There has been a recent surge of interest in growing vegetables, herbs, fruit and other edibles at home and I think that is great!

Some of this interest is coming from people who have previously grown their own food, but stopped because it seemed easier and cheaper to buy it. Others are totally new to the whole growing process and don't really know how to start, what they can grow or how they can grow it.

In this changing world, people have become much more aware of the fragility of our food supply and they want to feel some control. They want to feel that, if the worst happens they can, at least partially, provide for themselves and their loved ones!

As a long-term gardener, I really hope that those of you who are more recent gardeners "stay with the program" and learn the joy and excitement that comes from watching a seed or seedling transform into a plant that you can pick and eat. And, having discovered how vibrant and fresh home-grown vegetables are, and how good they taste, you will become more selective about the bland, tired vegetables you purchase!

That is the intention of this book. To give you the information you need to grow your own food in a simple, easy to use format that helps everyone: both new gardener's and long-term gardeners, to stay with this growing passion!

Especially when things go wrong! And sadly they will. Even experienced gardeners have failures! We have plants die, we have them attacked by pests and diseases, we have them with stunted growth for absolutely no reason. The important thing is to:

1. **Not give up**
2. **Figure out what went wrong so you don't repeat the mistake**
3. **Try and save the crop or plant in question if possible.**

To me, growing plants is exciting. And frustrating. And ultimately very fulfilling! I started my first garden at 6 years of age. However, it wasn't until years later when I had my own home, that I tried my hand at growing herbs. Then, after I had moved to the tropics and sub-tropics I tried growing vegetables and finally fruit!

I too have had times when I have found it easier to buy my vegetables at the farmers market or supermarket, but then you get back into the rhythm of growing your own herbs and vegetables and are reminded just how much better they taste. And, as a bonus, you can often grow different varieties to those you find in the stores.

If you have children or grandchildren, it is a great way of showing them where their food comes from and involving them in the process of growing some of their own foods. And, if you have a fussy eater in the family, many parents and grandparents have found that this is a great way of getting children to try new foods!

Whatever your motivation, you may not be sure how to start on this gardening venture, and you may not know who to ask. Your neighbour down the road may have a great garden, but when you talk to them about the garden, it's like they are talking another language and you feel inadequate because you can't recognize the plant names and don't know what tools or pests they are talking about, so you smile and walk away rather than ask any further questions. More about this language later!

You can join a Facebook group, and some of these are great, but I often find the advice contradictory...... which post do you believe?

If the above information resonates, then this book is for you! I have taken all those questions that you want to ask, and put them into this handy book in simple, easy text. I tell you how to prepare the soil, what tools you will require, and give you tips on what might go wrong and how to deal with that should it happen. It's the type of book I wished I'd had, especially when I wanted to grow vegetables and herbs that I could eat!

So, let's get into it! This book is designed to be used as a resource. You can sit down and read it from beginning to end, or you may just want to look up the answers for your immediate problem or question. I hope you find it valuable and that it answers all your questions as you start your own edible garden.

Chapter 2

HOW TO GET STARTED

This Chapter is about how to get started on your vegetable and herb garden

Jacko's first vegetable garden at 7 years of age
Alicia Rose

1. So, how do I get started?

You have decided you want to grow some vegetables. That is the first step towards getting started! It really is that simple! The next step is to decide where you want to put your garden, determine whether it gets enough sunlight and water for what you want to grow and then learn what will be the best vegetables to grow for your space.

There is a lot of information available on the internet. Some of it is great, some of it is confusing, some of it is so general it really doesn't provide enough guidance and some of it is very complex and seems to be speaking another language.

Even I get confused with some of the conflicting advice! And I get annoyed! I worry, especially for beginner gardeners who don't have the knowledge to go......hang on, that's not right.

You don't need to know a lot of this information. In fact, some of the best vegetables I have seen grown have been by novices! However, before you even think of buying any plants, seeds or seedlings, you do need to make a few choices.

These choices include deciding where you are going to plant your vegetables. Do you have a garden? Or are you living in a unit, townhouse or even a retirement village? Do you have a lot of space? Do the vegetables you want to grow need a lot of sun? Do they need a lot of water? Do you want to plant seeds or seedlings? Can you grow vegetables from off-cuts?

Making the right decisions about the best site, both for water and sunlight and the best vegetables to grow can save you time, money and energy. It can also save you from the disappointment of not having your plants grow.

2. What can I grow?

So, what can you grow? The first thing to know is: what you can grow is controlled by where you live. This is why you will hear people talking about growing zones, or asking where you live. What will grow easily in the tropics will really struggle, or won't grow at all, in a temperate or cold zone. Likewise what grows easily in summer probably won't grow, or may even die in winter!

There are plenty of easy-to-grow, fail-safe plants that you can grow. These include herbs like parsley, thyme, mint, oregano and marjoram, as well as vegetables such as radishes, lettuce, bok choy, spinach and silverbeet.

You could also choose some easy flowering plants such as marigolds, pansies and violets, which you can use in salads and as food decoration. These are also great as companion plants, to help keep the bugs away from your vegetables. More about that later.

There are enough easy-to-grow plants so you don't have to deal with the frustrations and disappointments that can come from tricky plants like artichoke or cauliflower, and yet still be considered the gardening superstar among your family and friends!

3. What tools and equipment do I need?

If you go into any nursery, garden centre or hardware store you will see a vast assortment of tools for use in the garden. There are even different choices within the tools, like several different types of spades and forks.

As a new gardener what do you really need to get started? If you only want to grow a few herbs indoors, then you really don't need any special tools. You can use an old fork from the kitchen to dig around the top of the pots and an old jug or bucket for watering your plants.

For a larger garden, you will need some basic tools. I suggest you start with a gardening fork, spade, trowel, gloves and secateurs. You will also need a few buckets from your laundry and some basics like seaweed solution, liquid and slow-release fertilisers.

As your gardening activities expand you can add additional tools such as hand saws, pruning saws, hedge trimmers, electric pruners, power planters and so on. The list is somewhat endless, depending on the size of your garden. I cover selection and purpose of many of these tools later in the book.

4. How long do vegetables and herbs take to grow?

Growing your own vegetables does take time. You can't expect to plant seedlings today and be picking beans or lettuce tomorrow. It will take at least 4 weeks before you can start harvesting something, depending on factors like plant selection, soil, water, season, climate, fertiliser etc. In late spring and summer you can start picking some herbs and vegetables such as lettuce, coriander and basil as soon as they are established and growing new leaves.

With vegetables like lettuce, bok choy and spinach, as well as herbs like basil, parsley, coriander and mint, this picking can start as quickly as 3-4 weeks depending on soil temperature, whether you planted seeds or seedlings and whether you have given the plant enough food and water. Other vegetables like kale, silverbeet, eggplant and tomatoes take longer, and generally can be harvested any time after about 8-10 weeks.

Asparagus, which is one of the only truly perennial vegetables, takes around 2 years to grow to the point where you can harvest the spears. To make up for this long lead time, asparagus can live in your garden for up to 25 years, producing spears each year, as long as you have grown it in the right spot and keep it fed and watered.

5. How much time will it take? And what takes up this time?

Your vegetable garden does require regular care and attention! It isn't a case of set and forget. However, the amount of time you put in will generally be rewarded by the amount of food that you grow for yourself and your family. You will need to allocate time for watering, fertilising, weeding, pest control, repotting and replanting.

The amount of time you need to set aside will depend on the size of your garden, what you plant and where you create your garden. If you only want a few pots indoors, or on a balcony, then it can take just a few minutes each day.

However, if you have a large garden and decide to grow some of your own vegetables, then it can take a few hours each week.

If you get really bitten by the gardening bug and decide to try your hand at full sustainability, growing most of your own fruit and vegetables, having chooks or other animals then it can absorb several hours daily. However, like everything, it is best to start small so you don't get overwhelmed!

The amount of time you spend watering your garden will also depend on what you are growing and the season. If you are growing Mediterranean herbs like rosemary, thyme and lavender then you probably only need to water once or twice a fortnight, but if you are growing vegetables in a bright sunny garden, you may need to water them every day or even twice a day in summer, and every 3 to 4 days in winter.

Weeding and pest control takes a few minutes every couple of days. If you get into a routine you will keep most weeds and bugs under control, which will save you time and effort in the long run. If you don't deal with pests and weeds as they appear, it only takes a short amount of time for these invaders to get out of control, which means your plants don't grow as well, and can lead to your plants dying as they collapse from the effects of a full-on pest attack.

You should plan on fertilising your plants approximately every 4-8 weeks, depending on the season. Most plants will benefit from a dose of liquid fertiliser between applications of a solid, slow release fertilizer.

6. Can I grow a healthy garden without any artificial fertilisers or poisons and not have the bugs out-compete me for my food?

I see people on Facebook asking about what fertiliser they need, or what pest is this and how do I control it? Then armed with this Facebook advice, they go to their local garden centre or hardware store to find shelves full of fertilisers, chemicals, soil additives, pest control and weed control products.

The good news is that you really can create a healthy, productive, growing garden without using many of these products at all!

A healthy garden begins with good soil! Healthy soils lead to healthy plants. Healthy plants are more resistant to insects and disease. So what to do if you don't have good soil? You don't need to go out and buy soil and sometimes, if you, do it can lead to more problems!

It is best to start with what you have. You can improve your soil by adding lots of organic matter. Organic matter is a nice way of saying dead and decomposing plant and animal material. To add organic matter can be as simple as not removing all the leaf litter from your garden, and by adding composts, manures and mulches to the soil, as these increase the soil's capacity to retain water and nutrients. Healthy soil also supports beneficial microbes and worms, which are essential to good plant growth.

Having good soil doesn't mean that you won't get any pests or diseases, just that you will have healthier plants that can survive these problems better. And there are many ways to deal with pests that don't involve reaching for a bottle of poison to spray them. I will deal with this later, but it is much better for your garden, and for you, to try to keep these bugs below damaging levels, so that natural predators can come into your garden and help clean them up. Natural predators include beneficial insects, spiders, bats, birds, lizards, and frogs.

I will deal with this later in the book, advising on how to improve your soil, create your own compost, what pests and diseases may be in your garden and how to deal with the damaging ones and encourage the good ones.

7. *What about organic gardening? How is this different to normal gardening?*

Organic gardening can be described as chemical-free gardening, earth-friendly gardening or natural gardening. A basic definition of organic gardening is "gardening without man-made fertilisers, pesticides and chemicals", or "gardening as nature intended". The problem with organic gardening is that, like anything else, there are many different viewpoints and different inclusions and exclusions.

You can find a lot of information about gardening organically or sustainably, using permaculture or moon planting or biodynamics. Isn't this just what normal gardening is you wonder? Isn't all gardening natural? And isn't what you grow just naturally better for you?

Sadly not all garden principles, or the products they recommend, are natural or even sustainable. And they can certainly, sometimes, not be healthy for you or your family or even your soil. This is why more people are turning to organic gardening and also to buying organic vegetables.

I prefer to utilise biological gardening practices, which is my version of organic gardening. Biological gardening is a method of gardening that supports the natural health of the whole environment or eco-system in which the garden resides.

A vegetable garden grown using biological gardening methods looks at providing an environment that supports and feeds the plants, worms, soil microbes and beneficial insects, rather than simply making plants grow. Research shows us that the flavour of fruit and vegetables is directly related to the quality of nutrition that the plant itself has enjoyed, and this is substantially better in a biologically healthy garden.

I have based the information and recommendations in this book on biological gardening practices, which I have tested and experimented with over many years and I have worked hard at putting this knowledge into as simple and straightforward language as possible.

8. *What about plant names? Why do people sound like they are speaking another language when they talk about plants?*

When you talk to friends or other gardeners about your garden, and what you are trying to grow, often they will start talking about plants that you have never heard of. They may even sound like they are talking a foreign language. Well the good news is, they are talking a foreign language. They are talking Latin! So, why are they doing this?

Every single plant on Earth has a unique name, which is known as its botanical name. Botanical names are generally based on Latin. You don't have to learn Latin to grow beautiful plants. And many gardeners, myself included, prefer to call plants by their common names.

However, the common name used in one country may refer to a totally different plant in another country, or even to different plants across States. This is where the botanical name can come in handy, as it ensures that everyone is talking about the same plant, regardless of where they are based in the world.

Latin or botanical names are a way of describing and cataloguing a plant, and it can tell you quite a lot about the plant, once you understand the system. For example a few of the common words used in botanical names can tell you:

Where a plant is from:

- *alpinus* = alpine regions,
- *canadensis* = from Canada,
- *chinensis* = from China,
- *japonica* = from Japan

The colour of flowers or foliage:

- *alba* = white,
- *aurea* = golden,
- *glauca* = blue,
- *rubra* = red

The shape of the plant:

- *arboreus* = treelike,
- *compactus* = compact or dense,
- *nanus* = dwarf,
- *scandens* = climbing

Understanding a bit about the botanical names and what they mean can be helpful when you are looking for advice on how to grow a plant, or when you are looking for a specific plant. In this age of the internet where you can be talking with gardener's way outside your local community, this can be very important, and even photos may not help you differentiate between plants.

So, when another gardener starts talking to you in a different language, know that they are probably using botanical names. This doesn't mean they are going to be a better gardener than you, just that they have taken a bit of time to learn the Latin-based names, which is why it sounds like they are speaking a different language.

Chapter 3

PLANNING AND PREPARING

This Chapter is about why and how to plan and prepare for your vegetable garden

Potential site for vegetable garden

9. How do I decide the best place for my vegetable garden?

So, where are you going to put your garden? When you walk outside, you may be faced with a backyard or front yard that is just an expanse of green. Maybe it's nice lawn or maybe, as I found in my current garden, just a vast expanse of weeds! Hopefully you will have one or two places where you can create an edible garden.

This will make it easier to decide where to put your garden, but it may make other choices a bit trickier depending on the conditions in that area.

If you have several areas to choose from, look at factors such as access to water, sunlight, big trees, fences, paths or paving. If you are trying to decide between a few different areas, I suggest you take a book or magazine outside and sit in the selected area for a few hours.

This will give you an idea of the amount of sun or shade the area gets, and whether your plants will thrive here. I find it best to choose a place that is seen whenever you go outside, as this will ensure the garden and plants will get some attention from you. We all know the old adage about being out of sight being out of mind! As a result, many gardening books will recommend that you grow your vegetables and herbs close to the house, a recommendation that I support.

Being close to the kitchen and being seen makes it easier to plan and use the harvest of herbs and vegetables you have grown and add them to your meals. However, that does depend on the amount of sunlight and access to water, which I will cover now.

10. How much sunlight do my plants need?

All plants require some sunlight, or good diffuse light, to grow and survive. If you want to grow edible plants such as vegetables, these normally require between 5 and 8 hours of sunlight a day. This is because vegetables and herbs are generally quick growing plants. In order to grow quickly, vegetable and herb plants need the nutrients they produce from photosynthesis. Without enough sunlight they cannot produce enough nutrients and therefore fail to grow.

Some green vegetables like lettuce and bok choy can grow and thrive with less sunlight, as long as they get around 3 hours of sunlight a day. Most vegetables and herbs will not grow in shaded gardens, despite what some websites and blogs might claim.

The quality of the sunlight is also important. Early morning or late afternoon sunlight is lower strength and therefore plants need more hours of this sunlight, compared with sunlight at midday, which is full strength.

11. Can a plant have too much sun?

Plants, like people, can actually get sunburnt! Some plants love growing in full sunlight and will struggle if they don't get sufficient sunlight. Other plants only grow in shade and will get sunburnt and even die when placed in full sun.

So, how do plants get sunburnt? The most obvious way is when you spray the leaves of a plant with pest oil and then have an unexpectedly hot day. The pest oil blocks the plants ability to breathe and you can kill a plant this way. I have lost a few plants over the years through incorrect application of pest oil!

Another way a plant may get sunburnt is when it is moved from a shaded position into a sunny position. This can happen when you buy a plant from a store or a nursery where it has been living in air-conditioning for some time.

These plants need to be slowly returned to outdoor conditions or else they can go into shock, get sunburnt or even frost-burnt if you live in a cold-climate zone. This re-introduction process is known as "hardening-off".

The process of hardening off involves moving the plant from a shaded spot through to a sunny position and it should be done in a couple of stages. Start by moving the plant from shade into a well lit position that is not in direct sunlight. After a few days in this position it will have adjusted and can be moved to an area where it gets some sun, preferably morning sun. I have laser light around my place so plants get lots of bright light without getting any direct sunlight. Otherwise the shade of a patio, tree or bush is ideal.

Once the plant has adjusted to morning sunlight, the amount of sunlight can be increased bit by bit until it can cope with all day sun. On really hot days or during heat-waves you may need to provide even heat-loving plants with temporary shade to protect them from sunburn. Temporary shade can be provided by shade-cloth or using large leaves like palm fronds. My "go-to" is using old umbrellas, as these keep the direct sun off while still allowing light through.

12. How much water will my vegetable garden need?

Without regular water plants die, so you need to make sure you have access to a reliable source of water that is easy to reach. This is usually not a problem on your average suburban block, but it can be an issue in a large garden, or a micro-garden on balconies, courtyards or roof gardens. In summer you need to water your vegetable garden every day, or even twice a day, so you want to make this as easy as possible. If it is difficult to do, then it becomes an onerous task, that you avoid and your plants and garden will suffer!

Although you probably want to start small, using a garden hose or even watering cans, down the track you might want to consider some sort of automated drip or sprinkler system for your garden. This can take the pressure off having to set time aside daily to water the vegetable garden.

Sprinkler and drip systems can be integrated into your garden when you are setting the garden up, or they can be retrofitted quite easily once you decide you are going to continue with growing your own vegetables. More on watering later in the book.

13. What else is growing in the area and why does it matter?

What else is growing in your garden can be an important determining factor when looking at where you intend putting your garden. If your garden has a couple of big trees then they will have big root systems. Even if you can find an area with enough sunlight, plants might still suffer because they are having to compete for their water and food with these trees. This is known as root competition.

That doesn't mean you will have to find another place for your garden, but you may need to put in a raised garden bed. If you do this you will also need some type of barrier to stop the roots invading your new garden. This can be as simple as old carpet (natural not synthetic!) or weed-mat. Both tree roots and weeds can be stifled with a weed-mat. Don't be tempted to use black plastic as this prevents the soil underneath the plastic from breathing, killing off the worms and microorganisms, until the soil turns sour!

This is also something to consider when planning your garden. When I was planning my current garden, I wanted privacy from neighbours, so planted several large shrubs and trees. These have grown and I now have plenty of privacy, but I have reduced the area where I can grow vegetables and herbs. It is always a trade-off!

14. What can I grow where I live?

When you are growing vegetables and herbs for the first time, start by considering what it is that you like to eat. For example, there is no point planting coriander if you don't enjoy the taste of it!

There are thousands of different types of plants available. Even if you are only interested in growing your own herbs, there are well over 100 different herbs for you to select from.

Unless you have a lot of spare time available, or are an experienced gardener, then it is best to aim for plants that are reliable and easy to grow. Luckily, most herbs and a lot of everyday vegetables are easy to grow and don't require a lot of care or attention in order to thrive and provide you with food.

When you think you know what you want to grow, you need to then determine whether it will it grow where you live? There are around seven growing zones across Australia and what zone you live in will determine what plants will grow easily, what plants will struggle and what plants just won't grow.

In the USA there are eleven different growing zones (known as plant hardiness zones). I tell you this so when you come across a website or blog that talks about "hardiness zone 11" you will know that you are on a site for growing vegetables in America. Nothing wrong with this, but I find it's hard enough getting my head around the requirements in my own garden without needing to understand the requirements of another zone half a world away!

In Australia, the zones are broadly divided into tropical, subtropical, warm, mild temperate, cool, alpine/cold and arid. It is important to know what zone you live in, as this will impact what you can grow and when. Some plants simply won't live long if you attempt to grow them in the wrong season, the wrong zone or in the wrong location.

This is a really important consideration when growing vegetables and herbs. You cannot grow frost sensitive plants like tomatoes or basil in winter if you live in a cool temperate or cold/alpine zone and you cannot grow broad beans, cauliflower, parsley or coriander in summer if you live in a tropical or sub-tropical zone.

Chapter 4

SOILS AND SUCCESS

This Chapter is about the most basic requirement, soil, and how to set your garden up for success from the start.

What good soil looks like

15. How do I know what type of soil I have?

As a gardener who is new to growing your own foods, the question of soil can seem a bit unnecessary and even strange. Isn't all dirt the same? And can't I just throw some seeds into the dirt and won't they just grow?

In fact, it can take even seasoned gardeners a long time to realise the benefits of preparing and looking after their soil. Many of the following principles will apply even if you just want to grow vegetables in pots or raised garden beds.

Firstly you need to find out what type of soil you have. Basically, there are 3 types of soil: Clay, Sand and Loam.

- Clay soils are heavy and retain water when it rains, and become rock-hard when dry so you will need to add more organic matter to open up the soil structure.

- Sandy soils are low in organic matter and allow water to drain right through them, so you will need to provide your plants with more water and more food or build up the organic matter in the soil.
- Loamy soils are soils that have the right amount of clay, organic matter and sand for plants to be able to grow and thrive, as the plants are able to access the greatest levels of nutrients and water.

If you want to know whether you have clay soil or sandy soil you can do a test by getting a glass of water, adding a teaspoon of soil and watching how long takes to settle. Sandy soils will settle pretty quickly, leaving clear water at the top, while clay soils will be cloudy for a lot longer.

Another method is to let a hose run for a few minutes on a patch of soil and see how long it takes to drain away. With sandy soils it will disappear almost immediately whereas with heavy clay soil it will puddle on the surface and make mud. You can follow this up by taking a teaspoon of the soil and squeezing it in your hand. When you open up you hand, does the soil separate and fall apart? Then it's primarily sandy soil. If it forms a nice loose ball, but isn't sticky then it's loam and if it forms a tight sticky ball, then it is primarily clay.

Finally you can ask at your local nursery. They can give very general advice. For example, Canberra in the Australian Capital Territory is mostly heavy clay, whereas Perth, Western Australia is mostly sandy soil.

I have gardened mostly on clay soils which I have turned into loam with much effort. So you can change your soil profile. The type of soil is important as some plants, such as avocadoes do not like clay soil. The biggest problem with clay soils is that if you get too much water it hangs around and can kill your plants by drowning their roots.

And when you don't get enough rain it can bake *really* hard, making it very difficult to plant things. With sandy soil on the other hand is difficult to keep water up to the plants whether you are having a drought or a flood!

16. What is soil pH and why is this important?

You may hear or read about the pH of the soil and not understand what pH means or whether it is important for you to know about. The pH is actually telling you whether your soil is acidic, alkaline or neutral.

The pH scale goes from 0 to 14, where pH 0 to 6 is acidic, pH 7 is the neutral point and pH 8 to 14 is alkaline. The pH scale is a logarithmic scale. What this means is that a difference of 1 point on the pH scale means that the soil is 10 times more acidic or alkaline!

The best way to determine your soil's acidity is to test your soil. Some nurseries will conduct the tests for you, or you can buy a simple soil testing kit from your local nursery or hardware store.

All you have to do is dig down about 5 to 10 cms and collect a teaspoon of the soil to conduct the measurement on. Place this teaspoon of soil on a mixing plate, add the pH Dye indicator and stir well. Then puff on some of the Barium Sulphate powder and read off the pH against the colour chart.

It is important that you dig down so that you are measuring the pH at the actual root zone of the plant as this is where the pH can affect the health of your plant. If you measure the pH at the surface of the soil you will not get an accurate result. It is also important that you run pH tests every few metres as the pH can change considerably over a very small distance.

17. What do I do if my soil tests as too acidic or too alkaline?

Most vegetables grow best in a slightly acid to neutral soil. Some herbs such as lavender, rosemary and oregano like slightly alkaline soils, but very few plants do well in a strongly acidic or alkaline soil.

This is because soils that are strongly acidic prevent the plants from getting enough nitrogen, phosphorus, or potassium even if these elements are available in the soil. Soils that are strongly alkaline prevent the plants from getting adequate amounts of iron, manganese and phosphorus, again even if these elements are present. This means that your plant could starve to death, even though you have added enough fertiliser, minerals and trace elements, because the plant cannot access these.

Finding that your soil is too acidic or too alkaline doesn't mean the end of your garden or your plans to grow your own vegetables. There are some easy remedies you can put into practice to bring the soil back within the desired range.

If you find that your soil is too alkaline then you need to add materials that are naturally acidic, as these will help bring it to the more neutral zone or slightly acidic range. Acidic materials you can use include coffee grounds or organic composted materials to reduce the alkalinity naturally. You can also add materials such as iron sulphate or organic sulphur in either liquid or powder form to help make the soil more acidic.

If you find that your soil is too acidic then you need to add lime or dolomite to bring it to a more neutral zone, which is optimum for plant growth. With acidic soils you can also add poultry manure or wood ash from wood fires to help reduce the acid levels.

You need to be careful with this, as a little goes a long way, and you don't want to go too far and end up with an alkaline soil. However, the benefit of using natural products like wood ash is that you will also be adding natural minerals and nutrients to your soil.

I prefer a slightly acidic soil as many of the plants I love to grow like eggplant, strawberries and blueberries prefer an acid soil. Plants that I know prefer a more alkaline soil, like mint, I grow in pots. This is also a great idea as mint can become a weed very quickly in the garden.

It is important to be cautious when trying to change the pH of your soil. The last thing you want is to go from one extreme to the other. It is best to adjust the pH a small amount at a time, over a period of several weeks, although this can be frustrating.

I have had times when a small change in one part of the garden has resulted in a sudden change of pH. Like when I had to put in a new pool fence and the contractor installing the fence used a lot of cement. Cement is lime based and very alkaline so it makes the surrounding soil alkaline as well. I lost several plants including a superbly performing blueberry!

And a note of caution. If all this seems too difficult, and you think it will be easier to just get a load of soil from the garden centre, do not assume that because you ordered "top of the range topsoil, suitable for growing vegetables", that it will be the correct pH.

I have heard of alarming stories of gardeners who ended up with soil with a high pH (one even as high as pH10.5, which is extremely alkaline) so absolutely nothing would grow. The gardener in question learnt a very expensive lesson, as none of the seedlings that he planted grew. They all died very quickly after being planted! So he not only had to pay for the soil, and the dead seedlings, but also for all the chemicals and mulches he needed to reduce the pH to a level where plants could grow!

18. How do I prepare the soil for my vegetable garden?

I am going to start with preparation of the soil as if you are going to develop a garden bed. Some of these principles will apply even if you just want to grow plants in pots or raised garden beds, and I will cover these in more detail later.

So, you have decided where you want to put your garden bed and it is currently covered in grass or weeds. The conventional way of getting rid of grass and weeds is to remove them by hand, but this can be a slow process requiring quite a lot of physical exertion, and this tends to put people off.

The quickest way to kill the grass and weeds off would be to spray with a Glyphosate-based weedkiller, such as the one's found on your local hardware store or nursery. The problem with this method is that, despite the name, weedkillers are not specific to weeds and will kill any plant they come in contact with. There is also emerging evidence that, despite claims to the contrary, these weedkiller chemicals remain in the soil and can impact the plants you try to grow later. This is not good if you want to eat the plants you grow, as you don't want to be eating poisoned vegetables!

This can make the conventional methods look more appealing. However, before you set aside a week of your holidays or go out and hire yourself a labourer to do this manual work for you, there are a few other options you can consider. These options all involve smothering the weeds, removing their access to air and/or sunlight in some way and killing them.

The first option involves covering the area for several weeks with a tarpaulin, heavy plastic or even a piece of old carpet. The tarpaulin is probably the least effective option as you need to weight it down and it takes several weeks to produce results.

If you use heavy clear plastic, you will also need to weight it down, but the clear plastic will actually bake the weeds and, in so doing, will also kill any weed-seeds that may be present in the soil.

This is best done in summer where the hours of sunlight are the longest. It also assumes that the area under the plastic gets plenty of direct sunlight. Once all the grass and weeds have died off you can then dig over the soil, add plenty of compost and fertiliser and prepare to plant up.

I have tried both the tarpaulin and the plastic baking method with varying degrees of success. I found that the easiest and most earth-friendly option, is to put layers of newspaper or cardboard, followed by a layer of compost or manure, then a layer of straw or sugar cane mulch and fertiliser directly over the grass and weeds.

You create several layers until the garden bed is at the desired height, finishing with a final layer of compost or soil which can be planted directly into. This is known as a lasagne or layered garden, and involves no digging or pulling weeds!

As long as you make the layers thick enough, the weeds underneath will be starved of water, oxygen and sunlight and they will die. The great thing about creating this type of garden is that you can plant straight into it, so you can be planting your vegetable seedlings after a weekend of work, rather than waiting several weeks for the Glyphosate to work or the labourer to remove the weeds!

A raised garden bed can also do away with the need to dig over the ground and remove all the weeds. All you do is construct the raised garden bed, whether it be from timber or one of the pre-constructed metal beds, place them in the selected position and fill them with a mix of soil and compost. Lasagne gardening can also be a great method to use to fill up the raised garden beds.

Remember, when positioning your raised garden beds be sure about their placement as, should you have to move their position or change the soil, it can be a time-consuming and laborious job, as you will have to dig all the soil out.

19. Why is it important to prepare the soil?

Generally if your soil is healthy, your plants will be healthy too! To get healthy soil, you need plenty of organic matter in the soil.

Organic matter is a nice way of saying you need decaying and dead plant materials, as these provide the necessary nutrients to the plants. It will also help to provide a better structure to your soil, allowing the soil to be looser and less compact.

The more organic matter you can add to your soil the better as, without organic material, your soil won't have worms or beneficial bacteria and it will easily become depleted of vital nutrients.

If you go out to your backyard now and try and insert a garden fork or spade or even a mattock into the soil where you plan to put your vegetable garden, the chances are that it will probably bounce off the surface! And possibly jar your arms and shoulders. I know, I have done this! There is nothing more frustrating to a gardener than to try and plunge a garden fork into a clay-based soil and have it go less than 2cm!

That is unless you are very lucky and it has previously been prepared as a garden bed. This is because the soil will not have been dug up for a long time. It will have become dense and compacted and will be lacking organic matter, oxygen and worms!

To be able to grow vegetables successfully you need soil that is healthy and alive with plenty of worms and their castings. You also need lots of bacteria and fungi. We have been taught to think of bacteria as bad, but they are actually vital to your soil and your plants (see Chapter 8 for more information).

When you are starting from scratch the simplest way to add organic material to your soil is to create a layered garden (see above). I learnt this the hard way and have variously used labourers, my own muscle power and rotary hoes to prepare the soil for a new garden bed.

Once you have the garden up and functioning, at the end of each season leave some plants to die back naturally. Remove any seed heads otherwise you may end up with an unwanted crop. Even if you don't remove seedheads, and you end up with an unwanted crop, instead of treating is as a disaster, use it! Let the plants grow to about 10 centimetres in height and then dig them back into the soil, as this will add even more organic material to your soil. This is a process known as "green manure" and some gardeners deliberately grow up a crop of green manure just to turn over into the soil.

Another other way of adding good organic material to your soil is to add some homemade compost and organic matter like sugar cane mulch to your garden. Instead of putting leaves and grass clippings into the rubbish bin, turn them into compost and add this to your soil on a regular basis (more on composting later).

You can put lawn clippings directly on to your garden, but you do need to be careful where you put this. The grass clippings can create quite a lot of heat as they decompose and break down, and the heat can "cook" any plants that they may be too close to. This is the primary reason why you will read not to put clippings too close to plant stems and tree trunks.

20. If I want to create a layered or lasagne garden, how thick should each layer be?

As I noted previously, one of the easiest ways to make a garden bed is using layers of compost, straw and manure. This adds all the necessary organic material easily without the need for heavy digging.

It may seem random to a new gardener, but there is a solid basis for the method of creating a layered garden. You need to alternate layers of "brown" material with layers of "green" material. Brown materials are things such as dried leaves, sugar cane mulch, pea-straw or straw, newspaper or cardboard and peat or manures. The green layers comprise lawn clippings, green leaves and garden trimmings as well as vegetable and kitchen scraps.

Make sure that any cardboard you use is not waxed as this will prevent the cardboard from breaking down and may lead to a waxy layer being added to your soil.

The brown layers should be about 3 times thicker than the green layers. This is because the brown layers contain lots of carbon but are much less nutrient dense, while the green layers contain lots of nitrogen and nutrients.

You don't need to be meticulous about the relative amount of brown to green layers, as the layers will very quickly start to break down and, as they do, your garden layers will shrink and join together. However, there should be more brown material than green material to ensure a good final product.

To start a lasagne garden, put down a brown layer of either cardboard or about ten sheets of newspaper directly on top of the grass or weeds in the area selected for the garden. This cardboard or newspaper should be laid end-to-end so that there are no exposed areas for weeds to grow through. Hose this layer with water to keep everything in place as, if there is any breeze at all, you will find the newspaper starts to blow away and it is frustrating and a little amusing to chase sheets of newspaper all over the garden! By watering you are also beginning the breakdown process.

Place about a 5 cm layer of mushroom compost or animal manure such as cow or sheep manure on top of the cardboard/newspaper layer. Be careful with mushroom compost as it can be quite alkaline as mushroom farmers add salt to kill off the mushroom spores. I generally prefer to use cow or horse manure as this is still cheaply available at farm gates around the Redlands where I live. To the next layer, add about 10 cm of sugar cane mulch/pea straw/straw/lucerne hay or dried leaves. Then apply several handfuls of slow release organic fertiliser (see Chapter 6, Question 45-46) and water the layers again. Cover with a layer of grass clippings, kitchen vegetable scraps and garden pruning's to about 2 cm depth.

You need to repeat these layers until the bed is about half a metre high. Although this may look higher than what you had planned for, you will be surprised by how much this will shrink down in a few weeks as the materials decompose and the earthworms, bacteria and microorganisms get to work.

By following this method you have effectively created a hot compost heap. You should let the layers break down and start to decompose before planting up. However, if you don't want to wait, you can plant into the garden bed immediately, as long as your final layer is a layer of around 5 cm of good topsoil or home-made compost. You can plant seedlings or seeds into this layer immediately. As the plants grow, their roots will burrow down into the decomposing layers below, allowing them to access all the lovely nutrients as the decomposition process makes them available. Try it, it works!

21. What about soil temperature?

All plants have an optimum temperature range which they like to grow in. If the soil temperature is higher or lower than what the plant needs, then this will negatively affect plant growth. It's a bit like humans. Some of us dislike being cold, while others dislike being too hot!

The temperature most favourable for plant growth varies from plant to plant. If all plants had the same temperature requirements we wouldn't have plants growing in the different climate zones across the world. Many plants that grow in a cold climate survive by going dormant in winter, when the soil temperature drops below around 5° C, while other plants go dormant in the middle of summer in the tropics and won't grow until the soil temperature drops down a bit.

Some plants have adapted to include these temperature preferences into their lifecycle. As a result, many flowering bulbs and even many stone-fruit trees won't flower and form fruit if they don't get their winter chill.

This can be really challenging if you want to grow a plant outside the plant's preferred temperature range. For example, most stone fruits like cherries and apricots require a winter chill to set fruit. If you live in the sub-tropics like I do, then you have to find alternatives, although plant breeders have come a long way in finding low chill nectarines and peaches.

Soil temperature is also important when growing vegetables. If you sow seeds of summer growing plants before the soil is warm enough, they will fail to germinate. Likewise, if you plant seedlings for summer vegetables before the soil is warm enough, their growth will be very slow and spindly and they may die before the soil warms up enough for them to thrive.

When I was living in a cold climate I, like most other keen gardeners, would start my seeds off indoors or in greenhouses or cold-frames, to provide a warmer soil for the seeds. This meant that my tomatoes and basil could get a head start when I planted these seedlings outside once the soil temperature had risen enough for the plants to grow and thrive. Sometimes this is the only way to get a long enough growing season to produce a reasonable crop of tomatoes, basil and strawberries and make growing your own food viable.

Similarly, plants will generally stop growing, and may even die, if the soil temperature rises about 25-30° C, which can make growing some vegetables tricky in summer in many parts of Australia during heat waves. To help your plants survive it is important to protect the soil with mulches, sugar cane or decomposing leaf litter and compost to keep the soil temperature, and therefore the roots, cooler than 25 degrees.

Likewise, if your soil is too warm it will also affect seed germination and seedling growth. In the sub-tropics you have to wait until the soil temperature has dropped in autumn before you can plant the seeds and seedlings of many winter vegetables such as peas, cauliflower, broccoli or broad beans.

If you plant before the soil temperature has reached the correct temperature, the seeds will fail to germinate and may even "cook" in the soil. Any seedlings that you plant may bolt straight to flower and seed without actually producing the leaves that you want. Again, starting them off inside or in a greenhouse where you can better control the temperature allows you to get a head start.

Plants will also be affected by the temperature of the surrounding air. The optimum temperature for photosynthesis (the process by which plants create the sugars they need to grow) is around 25°C. Temperatures higher than this can actually cause the plant to cease production of the sugars that it needs to survive.

Higher temperatures in the surrounding air can also increase the amount of moisture a plant loses from its leaves. You will see plants wilt on really hot days as they lose moisture and you will need to help these plants survive by providing water to replace the moisture they have lost.

22. Is it better to plant in pots, raised garden planters, raised beds or in the ground?

This will depend to some extent upon your situation. If you are living in an apartment block, townhouse or even a retirement village without adjacent land then your choice will be limited to pots, vertical gardens or maybe a raised garden planter on a stand or wheels.

Even though I live on quite a large suburban block I use a mixture of pots, raised garden beds, normal garden beds and planters. This allows me to better control the soil and temperature requirements of individual plants, and to move them around as the sunlight changes from season to season. This approach also provides visual interest with plants at differing levels and positions, making the garden more intriguing.

So, like me, even if you have space available you may decide to use pots, raised planters or raised garden beds. Raised garden planters are a great option if you only have a small area, like a paved courtyard in a townhouse, or if you are renting and want to take your vegetables and herbs with you should you move.

Raised garden planters are also really beneficial for those that struggle to bend over, or have limited strength and movement. They can also be of enormous benefit to older gardeners and people in wheelchairs who still want to garden.

There are several types of raised garden planters available from your local nursery or hardware store. If you are handy with the tools (or know someone who is) you can make a raised garden from timber or plastic or metal. Just be careful to ensure that you only use untreated timber as you don't want chemicals like arsenic or lead leaching into your soil and maybe into your vegetables.

You can make really cheap raised gardens using recycled polystyrene boxes, which you can get for free from fruit and vegetable shops or fish shops. I have used these, even though there is some concern about whether the chemicals used to make polystyrene leach into the soils as they break down.

I use home-made compost, if I can get enough, or good quality potting mix to fill my pots and raised garden beds. Normal garden soil is generally too fine and can easily become compacted, which can result in water not getting absorbed properly.

Garden soil is also heavier than compost or potting mix, and it will make any pots very heavy when they are planted up. It is best to get it right the first time as you don't want to give yourself a back injury trying to move a pot full of soil to a new location.

So, which potting mix do you use? When you go to a garden nursery or hardware store you will find several different types of bagged-up potting mixes to choose from, and a range of prices. As a new gardener, it can be hard to know which one to choose.

That said, you generally get what you pay for!

So, although it may seem better value to buy a cheap potting mix, if you do this you will have to give your vegetables and herbs a lot more fertiliser, organic matter and nutrients than you will if you buy a more expensive potting mix, which contains more fertiliser and organic material. This is because cheaper potting mixes contain less food and composted organic material to support your plants.

You may also need to water the pots more frequently as, with less organic matter, there is nothing holding the water close to the plants roots, and the water will drain away, taking all the nutrients away from your plants.

It took me quite a while to learn this lesson. Now when I have to buy potting mix or compost, I buy the top of the range as it actually costs less in the long run when you factor in fertiliser, plant loss and slow growth versus rapid healthy growth.

If you decide to plant directly in the ground, you will avoid some of the costs associated with buying potting mix and raised beds, but you will still have the costs associated with preparing the ground, adding organic compost or manure and fertilising.

Chapter 5

PLANTING YOUR VEGETABLE GARDEN

This Chapter is about how to plant up your vegetable and herb garden.

Marigolds, beans, basil and capsicum planted together
Rohanne Young

23. When do I plant my vegetables?

Spring is normally considered the planting season for vegetables and herbs. This is because plants commence a growth spurt as the weather warms up, and the seeds or seedlings you plant will grow quickly.

Depending on which climate zone you live in, some vegetables and herbs will grow all year round. Other vegetables and herbs may prefer to grow only in summer or winter. I live in the sub-tropics, so autumn and winter are our best times for growing many vegetables and herbs including tomatoes, cauliflower, broad beans, basil, coriander, parsley, sage, dill and mint.

However, when I lived in the southern Australian states, with a cool or temperate growing zone, these vegetables and herbs need to be planted in spring for summer growing. I would have to start all my seedlings indoors, and only plant them out once the danger of frost had passed. This was normally after the full moon in October. Up until then, regardless of how warm the days have become, there was still the danger of a rogue frost!

A lot of herbs, and vegetables such as lettuce and radishes will also grow happily inside on a sunny windowsill or on a sunny balcony, often all year round. This is great if you want to grow some basil or coriander in the middle of winter and you live in a cool temperate climate, although you do need to take care as I have had some herbs die from frostbite even when growing inside on a windowsill.

Many people also plant new seedlings in autumn, while the soil is still warm and the plants can become established before the colder weather sets in.

24. How do I plant my vegetables?

Planting and transplanting vegetables is easy as long as you follow a few simple rules. I have already covered information like what type of soil or potting mix will be best for your plant, the best site and whether the water, sunlight and fertiliser needs can be met in the position you wish to grow your vegetables and herbs.

These steps are the same whether you are planting into a pot, raised planter, raised bed or into the garden. After you have prepared the site, you need to make a hole which, as a rule should be double the size of the root ball of the plant you are going to place in the hole. When I am planting up, I add a small amount of organic fertiliser in the hole where I am going to place the plant and cover it with a dusting of soil or compost to prevent the roots getting burned on contact.

I then place the plant in the centre of the hole and gently backfill with potting mix or compost or soil. By having a hole larger than the plant's root ball you ensure that the plant has some fresh loose soil to grow its roots into. This allows your plants to become better established before they hit the harder more compacted soil, which can slow your plant's growth considerably.

I have found that most seedlings and even shrubs like a lemon or lime tree, benefit if you gently tease a few of the roots loose from the root ball. This can be done just with your fingers and is particularly beneficial if the plant is root-bound i.e. the roots of the seedling or tree are tightly wrapped around themselves.

This will help the plant to start spreading its roots out into the soil in its new location. If you don't do this, you may find that the plant dies. I have, on occasion dug up a dead plant to find the roots still tightly wound with no new roots having grown out into the surrounding soil.

After I have planted my seedlings, I water my vegetables and herbs immediately with a seaweed solution, which is a tonic that helps to reduce transplant shock and to encourage root growth. The surrounding garden and soil also benefit from this application of water and seaweed solution.

25. What is the difference between annuals and perennials?

A lot of people get confused about annual and perennial plants. Although I grew up knowing the distinction, I can understand the confusion. You would think that plants that come back each year would be annuals, i.e. they grow annually, but this is not the case. Annual plants are those plants that grow from a seed, grow leaves, grow a flower that then produces seeds and then dies, all within one growing season or year.

This means they need to be replanted each spring or summer or autumn. And while you may have purchased them as seedlings, not seeds, this just means that someone has done the hard work of planting and growing the seeds until they grew into the seedlings you purchased.

The majority of vegetables and herbs that you are likely to grow, including lettuce, beans, peas, broccoli, bok choy, basil, coriander and even tomatoes fall into the category of being annuals. Some vegetables are naturally biennial, which means that they actually take two years to grow, flower, produce fruit or seeds and die.

On the other hand, plants that live for more than two years without needing to grow more from seed are called perennials. Although they may die down in winter, they will return each spring. Rosemary and lavender are examples of herbs that are perennials, while asparagus is one of the few vegetables that is a true perennial.

In the tropics and sub-tropics I find a number of vegetables that are classed as annuals are actually biennials that can live and produce for more than one year. This includes capsicum, eggplant and chillies. Although many gardeners replace them each year I have found that I get healthier, tastier fruits from older plants so I prefer to prune, feed, water and encourage my capsicums and chillies to live and bear fruit for two or more years.

26. Which is better to grow: seeds or seedlings?

Whether you decide to plant seeds or seedlings depends to some extent on how much money you want to spend on your herb or vegetable garden, what season it is and how quickly you want to be picking and eating your vegetables and herbs.

When I first started growing my own vegetables I would always buy seedlings, as I felt they were a better return on investment, they grew quickly so I could be picking and eating my vegetables in weeks. However, I soon found out that I had an overabundance of say tomatoes just at the time when they are cheapest to buy in the shops.

So I started to look for different varieties to those that would be selling in the supermarket or green grocer. This led me to grow more heritage vegetables and these aren't often available as seedlings in the nursery.

Heritage seeds, sometimes called heirloom seeds are those plants that have been grown and passed from generation to generation because of their diverse characteristics including colour, texture, taste, pest and disease resistance, as well as their suitability to local conditions. Heritage seeds are open pollinated, which means that they are pollinated by insects or wind, which helps the pollen from one plant to be transferred to the stigma of another nearby plant. If the plants are the same or similar variety, fertilisation will take place, leading to the creation of new seeds.

Vegetables that are not heritage or heirloom may also be pollinated and produce seeds, but there is no guarantee that the plant which grows from these seeds will be the same as the mother plant. That is another reason that I love growing heritage seeds, because when one of my plants goes to seed, I know that the new seedlings will grow true to the old plant.

Seeds do take a little longer to grow, but they also end up being better value for money. Not only do you get more than 10 times the number of seeds, and therefore plants, for approximately the same price as one punnet of seedlings, but also you can also get different vegetables from the ones that you find in the shops.

My friends have found that seeds are a great way to introduce their children and grandchildren to the joy of growing their own food. When using seeds in this way it is best to go for quick growing plants like lettuce or radishes, as the few days that seeds take to germinate can seem like a long time to young children.

Seedlings are a better option when I want to establish plants quickly, and also when I am planting vegetables and herbs in winter and early spring, as seeds will take longer to germinate when the soil temperature is cooler. This has become less of an issue since I started growing my own seedlings. When I am growing root vegetables like carrots and beetroot I find it best to sow them directly where I want them to grow as these plants dislike being moved, and can die off as a result of being transplanted.

When you are transplanting seedlings, be careful that you hold them by their root ball, not their stem as this can bruise or even crush their main growth tip.

I actually find it easiest to rest the stem of the seedling between my index and second finger while I tease the root ball out of the container. This ensures that I don't put any pressure on the stem of the seedling or plant.

Once you have transplanted your vegetable seedlings, again water them immediately with a seaweed solution to reduce transplant shock and encourage root growth. This will help them settle in faster, as the seaweed feeds microorganisms in the soil, which will help increase the number of seedlings that survive.

27. How do I sow seeds and how deeply do I plant the seeds?

Vegetable seeds come in all shapes and sizes from large seeds, like watermelon and pumpkin, through to tiny seeds like lettuce, celery and watercress. Large seeds are generally easy to handle, and easy to space out.

When you are first starting out, the seed packet will tell you how far apart to place your seeds and how deeply you should plant them. You should follow these directions, so that you leave enough room for the plant to grow without being crowded or having to compete with other plants. Once you have been growing vegetables for a while, it becomes automatic to space seeds and seedlings at roughly the right distance apart. You may notice this on some gardening shows where the presenter plants seeds without explaining why they are spacing the seeds so far apart.

Some vegetables and herbs have really small seeds, so you don't want to bury them too deeply, as chances are they won't be able to find their way to the surface to grow. The general rule is that you sow seeds only as deeply as twice the maximum width of the seed.

When you are planting seeds that are really small, it can be frustrating trying to make sure that all the seeds don't end up in the one hole. I mean, apart from being wasteful, it just means that you are going have to thin the seedlings out later. However, there are a few things you can do to make sure that your seeds are nicely spaced.

The method I use is to mix the seeds with fine sand in a glass jar with a hole punched in the lid. When shaken together the sand will help disperse the seeds so that only a few seeds land in each hole or are well spaced along the row. Cover the seed/sand mix with a light covering of soil and water well. Alternatively, instead of using a glass jar, you can use an old salt shaker, with the sand-seed mix, and treat it just like you are seasoning your dinner.

Another option is to use seed tape, where the seeds have been fixed onto a strip of bio-degradable tape at fixed distances. The tape is placed in the prepared row and covered with a light cover of soil. I don't normally bother with seed tape as I know approximately how closely I want to plant my seeds. However, if you want to use this method seed tapes are becoming more available commercially, or you can make your own using paper towelling and a glue of flour and water to fasten the seeds.

Some gardeners don't worry about how closely the seeds are, and thin them out as the seedlings emerge. I find this a bit wasteful as quite a lot of the seedlings die off due to competition for food and soil.

However, it is useful when growing root vegetables like carrots, as you get to harvest some carrots as young sweet carrots, which then makes room for the remaining seedlings to grow into mature, larger carrots.

When I am planting vegetable seeds I normally cover them with a very fine layer of soil or seed-raising mix. With many seeds, the main reason for covering them is to ensure that you get a crop, instead of having all the seed eaten by hungry birds. I mean, in nature, which we are trying to copy, seeds that are transported by the wind land on the soil and grow without being covered in any way.

Larger seeds can dry out if they are not planted a bit deeper. However, I have grown many pumpkin and tomato vines as a result of these seeds being spread on the garden along with compost from the compost bin.

28. Should I grow my seeds in punnets or straight in the ground?

All herb and vegetable seeds can be planted directly into the vegetable patch. Other seeds are easier to start off in punnets or seed trays, so you can control the environment they start growing in to ensure better germination.

I used to sow the seeds straight into my vegetable garden and then get frustrated because nothing would show up, so I started growing the seeds in seedling trays and I have noticed a much higher success rate.

Mind you it took quite a while to be convinced, including a long period of buying seedlings from my local nursery. Growing more heritage crops also helped me change my way of planting seeds and seedlings.

When growing your own seedlings there are many different containers that you can repurpose, including old punnets and plastic pots, peat pots and even old egg cartons and the inner roll of toilet tissues. When using old punnets and pots, I make sure that I clean them well to prevent diseases getting into my new plants. This can be done by washing them thoroughly in warm water with a small amount of bleach added and then rinsing thoroughly.

For plants that don't like their roots disturbed like carrots and beetroot I find it better to make little pots that will decompose in the ground. These can be made from toilet roll inserts or egg cartons or even newspapers. Old egg cartons are a great option. You can break the carton apart and plant the seedling and carton directly into the vegetable garden without disturbing the roots.

I steer clear of the commercial peat pots as I have found that they don't break down nearly as easily as promised, and can become a prison for your seedling's root system. They prevent the roots being able to seek out food and water outside of the little peat pot and this can result in the plant dying.

Planting the seeds is exactly as outlined above (refer Question 27). A simple trick that I have found really useful is to soak the seeds in a dilute seaweed solution overnight before planting them in your preferred seed-raising mix filled container.

Keep the seed raising mix moist, but not too wet and wait until the new seedlings start to emerge.

When they have started to grow their second and third sets of leaves you can either plant them out into well-prepared soil in the garden, or pot them into a larger container with potting mix. I find that it is better to plant out half the seedlings into the garden and the other half into a bigger pot. The ones in the pot will generally grow slower, so I can transplant them in the garden a week or two later. This lets me stagger the planting so I get a more continuous crop, rather than a feast followed by a famine.

Whatever containers you decide to use, make sure that water can drain easily. Shallow containers are best for seed raising, as the seedlings really don't need a huge root zone and you will be planting them in the garden or larger pot before they fill up the little pod area.

Most seed packets will give you all the information you require about planting depth, seasonal sowing times, climate zones and the length of time between sowing, seeing the first tiny shoots appear and when you can expect to harvest your food.

29. Do I have to use commercial seed-raising mix?

Seed raising mix is lighter and looser than soil, so the seed gets a chance to germinate and push its roots and leaves through a lighter medium than soil. I prefer to make my own seed raising mix by combining equal parts of coir peat with propagating sand, vermiculite or perlite in a large bucket, or wheel barrow if you are planning on growing a lot of seedlings.

If you are only growing a few seedlings or are new to this process, commercial seed-raising mix is available and is a great option. It has been specially prepared for new seeds and should be sterile and free of disease if unopened. This ensures your seeds the best chance of germinating and growing without the risk of soil borne diseases, which can cause things like damping off. It can be really disheartening to have your seeds emerge healthy from the soil only to have them fall over and get all mushy and dead for no apparent reason.

30. What about a glasshouse? I've seen them on TV. Do I need one to grow seeds?

A glasshouse can be a great way to keep seeds warm, and to control the environment, while you are waiting for your seedlings to emerge. This can be important if the area you live in has extremes of temperature, such as cold nights or even potential frosts. However, you don't need to spend huge amounts of money to create a glasshouse.

I don't have a formal glasshouse structure. I don't really need one living in the sub-tropics. However, when I do want to provide seedlings or a cutting with extra protection I create a simple glasshouse using the top of a plastic bottle with the bottom cut off.

If I need space for more than one plant or punnet, I use a styrofoam box with a piece of glass over it. I repurpose a piece of glass from old picture frames that I buy for a few dollars from my local Op Shops. You can also use old 2-3 litre fruit juice containers, which you cut almost in half. Plant your seedlings in the bottom and close the top over. The plastic punnets that you buy cherry tomatoes and berries in, are also great for this purpose.

It is important to keep the seeds in their temporary glasshouses out of direct midday sun as you could burn your young plants as they emerge. And always handle glass with extreme care to ensure you do not sustain any injuries.

31. *Why do I need to thin out my seedlings?*

When you buy seedlings, and even when you have grown your own, you will often find several seedlings growing together in each punnet cell. In the past I used to think it easier to just plant all the seedlings together. However, I have found that it really is better to gently tease them apart and plant them out separately.

This is because if you plant the seedlings too close together they have to compete with each other for food, water and nutrients. This means you will get a poorer yield than if you placed them further apart where they don't have to compete. Also, research has shown that some plants release hormones that actively inhibit the growth of nearby plants.

Also, if you plant the vegetable and herb seedlings too close together, it can lead to fungal diseases such as damping off. This could result in you losing all your seedlings, and not just those that may be damaged when you are teasing them apart.

As a reward for taking the time to separate out the seedlings you end up with more plants to harvest. I am constantly amazed at how often a fairly weak looking little seedling will thrive once it has its own space in the vegetable garden.

32. *Can I strike a plant from a cutting instead of seeds?*

Cuttings are a great way of increasing your number of plants for little or no cost. I haven't had to purchase a rosemary bush since I discovered this trick! Cuttings are also a great way to grow plants that you are having trouble finding as a seed or seedling.

In fact, many herbs including basil, sage and oregano will grow roots when the cutting is placed in water on a windowsill or other brightly lit surface. Later you can take the rooted cutting and pot it up in potting mix or plant it straight in the garden.

I have seen many posts about growing rosemary in water, but until recently I had not had any success with this method. I have discovered that the secret is to use an opaque glass or bottle so that the roots can form easily in the dark.

However, I usually strike my rosemary plants from cuttings. To do this you need an established plant to take cuttings from, some sharp scissors or secateurs, honey, seed raising mix (see Question 30 above), a plastic plant pot and a plastic drink bottle.

I try and use "heel" cuttings as I find they have the greatest success. To get a heel cutting, find a small stem on the plant that you want to grow your new plant from, and gently pull this stem sideways until it breaks away from the main branch.

You will see that a small slice of the main branch has come away with the stem and this is called a "heel" cutting. The plant will actively produce new roots where this heel and the stem met.

Next, remove some of the leaves on the cuttings, so that only two or three leaves remain. You need to keep some leaves or the cutting will die before it can grow any roots.

Put your seed raising mix in a clean, plastic pot. Dip the cutting, heel end, in the honey. The honey acts as food and promotes growth as well as having anti-microbial properties that stop the plant being attacked by soil bacteria and dying.

Using a pencil or similar item, I make a hole in the potting medium and push the cutting into the hole, taking care not to rub off the honey. Gently press the potting medium around the stem with your fingers until it is supported. The cutting should not be more than half covered.

Next make a mini-greenhouse with the plastic bottle by removing the bottom with a sharp knife and carefully covering the cutting with the top of the plastic bottle. Water the pot gently, attach a label and place in a cool area out of direct sun, but with plenty of bright light.

I find the cuttings take root within a month or so, depending on the plant. You will know when the cutting has taken as it starts to grow new leaves. If you want to put several cuttings in a larger pot, that's fine. Just make sure you plant them about 5 cm deep and leave about 2-3 cm space between cuttings. On occasion I have found when doing this that I nearly lost all the cuttings, as the roots intertwined and the plants started to compete with each other. To prevent this, you may need to transplant these cuttings sooner.

When the cuttings have sufficient new growth they can be potted up into a larger pot. Give them some half strength liquid fertilizer at this point to encourage growth. I don't place the cuttings in the garden at this stage as I find they don't have enough of a root system to be able to feed themselves.

33. Can I re-grow vegetables from off-cuts?

I have seen posts on Facebook and YouTube about growing plants from off-cuts of purchased vegetables. In my experience a few of these do really well, but not nearly as many as the posts would have you believe.

For example, if you grow a carrot top, all you will end up with is green carrot tops. It won't regrow the carrot base. While this can be fun for kids to learn, you don't end up with an edible plant. Celery does regrow, but in my experience not nearly as robustly as the original celery that you purchased.

I have managed to grow sweet potatoes by planting the ends of a sweet potato that has started to shoot in the cupboard. I have similarly had some success with potatoes and shallots.

Some plants are really fun to grow from off-cuts though. One I get enjoyment from is the tops of pineapples. I cut the top off the pineapple, remove any fruit and the bottom few leaves. When doing this you often see where the new roots will form from. I just place these tops straight in the garden or in a large pot in a sunny spot. Within 18 months I am harvesting fresh, home-grown pineapples. This is great repurposing, as the top was just going to be thrown away. Besides it would have cost you about $20 to buy a pineapple plant at a nursery.

Chapter 6

WHAT CAN YOU GROW IN YOUR ENVIRONMENT

This Chapter is about what you can grow in your vegetable garden no matter what your environment

Some of Andrew's vertical garden
Rohanne Young

34. I only have a tiny amount of space. Can I grow vegetables or herbs?

With increasing urbanisation, residential blocks are getting smaller and more and more people are living in units, apartments and townhouses. This has given rise to a lot of really innovative methods to maximise gardening space in small gardens, courtyards and balconies. This means that you can grow many things, especially herbs and vegetables in a tiny amount of space.

The requirements I have outlined previously still apply i.e. plenty of sunlight and water, and this can be a bit tricky depending on the shade cast by nearby buildings. However, assuming enough sunlight and water you will be amazed at the amount of vegetables, herbs and even fruit that you can grow in a small area.

One of the best innovations is a vertical garden, where a frame is placed against a wall and pots containing herbs, vegetables and even flowers can be potted up and attached to the frame. This will give you a green wall, which can provide plenty of food from a small space. When setting these up I find it best to incorporate a drip water system into the design. Most of the pots are pretty small and can dry out quickly in summer, meaning that the lettuce you were going to use for dinner that night is now fried and crispy.

There are also vertical garden frames on wheels, which can be moved around the courtyard or garden to capture the maximum available sunlight. Make sure that you buy one that is sturdy enough, as the structure can get quite heavy once it is planted up with lots of potting mix and seedlings. And again, make sure you include some method of watering your herbs and vegetables. Depending on the height of your vertical garden you may need to install a small pump to help the water get to all the plants.

You can create your own vertical wall using hessian pockets for plants, old drawers or even hanging plastic bottles filled with soil and plants. Bear in mind that these vertical walls will all be relatively short-lived structures, as these materials will break down over time due to sun and water exposure. I have used plastic bottles and found they became very brittle and started to drop from their hangers after a single summer.

You can also create a frame from old pallets, but make sure you only use pallets where the wood has been heat treated, not the ones that have been treated with chemicals such as methyl bromide, as this can leach into the soil and be taken up by the veggies you are growing. Pallets are clearly marked with either HT, meaning "Heat treated" or MB meaning treated with Methyl Bromide. Only use HT pallets in your garden.

There are also tiered or tower gardens, where pots are placed in layers so that they provide a maximum planting space while taking up minimum area. You can either buy a commercial product or create your own using various sizes of plastic or terracotta pots.

As with growing herbs and vegetables in pots, you need to use a good quality potting mix in your vertical or tiered garden and you need to apply liquid fertiliser every 2 weeks to help your plants grow and thrive.

With any vertical garden make sure that you include a drip tray to stop the floor on your balcony or in your courtyard from becoming slimy from water and soil/fertiliser run-off.

35. What vegetables and herbs can I grow on a balcony?

When I was living in Townsville a friend of mine lived in a unit which had a reasonable sized balcony. I was amazed at the plants that she managed to grow on this balcony. There was a Pawpaw tree in a large pot and a lime tree in another pot. In between she had pots full of lettuce, bok choy and herbs including coriander and mint. A cherry tomato was trained up the railings. All the plants, including the pawpaw tree produced fruit. It just goes to show that many of the plants you can grow in a garden can also be grown on your balcony.

As with any garden, what you can grow is going to depend on the position of your balcony. Does it get any sun, does it get too much sun, does it get too windy and do you have easy access to water? If your balcony is in constant shade then there are very few edible plants that you will be able to grow on your balcony (see Question 38 for more information).

If your balcony gets a good amount of sun without getting baked, you can grow herbs, many vegetables and even a fruit tree like a lime or lemon in a large pot. Even if your balcony does get scorched by too much sun, you might consider putting up shade cloth or a trellis to reduce the severity of the sun and make the balcony a useable growing space.

The only limiting factors here will be your budget, the amount of space, access to water and your imagination. The question of space is becoming much less of a problem with some of the innovative developments in vertical gardens, which allow plenty of vegetables and herbs to be grown up a wall (see Question 34).

You can also explore using pots on metal shelves or even an old bookshelf. A tower garden made from different sizes of terracotta pots, filled with potting mix and stacked on top of each other can look fantastic without taking up too much of your balcony.

36. What herbs and vegetables can I grow indoors?

When I was at university the kitchen window of our flat got all the morning sun and I used to grow herbs in pots on that window sill. If I went back now, with everything I have learnt since then, that windowsill would be very productive! I would probably have 2 or 3 curtain rods across the window and hang pots of herbs and vegetables from each of the rods.

So, if you have a windowsill that gets full morning or afternoon sun, and you want to, you can definitely grow a number of herbs and several different types of vegetables indoors.

Personally, I think herbs are a better choice, as you get a lot more value from less space. Also, you can snip the herbs straight into what you are cooking.

My top 12 picks for edible indoor plants would include (depending on your taste preferences):

- chives
- coriander or cilantro
- sage
- perennial basil
- sawtooth or perennial coriander
- parsley, both curly and Italian or flat
- thyme
- mint
- oregano
- tarragon
- Vietnamese mint
- A Bay tree.

Most of these plants, except the Bay tree, will grow indoors on a sunny windowsill. The Bay tree grows into a large attractive shrub and should be grown in a large pot in a position where it can get several hours of sunlight a day.

All these plants should be considered temporary house guests and will perform best if they are allowed to rest outside when the weather permits. With the exception of the Bay tree, all these herbs should be considered annuals when grown indoors.

37. What can I grow if I only have a shaded garden? Can I grow any edible plants

I am actually finding shade more and more of a problem in my own garden, as the trees that I planted to give me summer shade and privacy have all grown. They do exactly what I wanted them to do. I just hadn't thought through the fact that they would also create shade on my vegetable and fruit gardens.

This has limited some of the choices I have for growing vegetables and I have had to make some changes. For example, I now have some large pots out the front of my house so that I can grow capsicum and chilli.

However, if your only position for a vegetable garden is in full shade, then the range of vegetables and herbs that you can grow will be severely restricted.

As I said previously, I get annoyed with internet posts that say things like "Top 10 vegetables you can grow in the shade", when they really mean only a few hours sunlight a day.........that is not shade!

Almost all vegetables need at least some direct sunlight to grow. If you only have shade in your garden there may still be a few options. These include planting in pots or planters that you can move around to capture whatever sunlight is available.

Also, you may find that while the ground is shaded, there is some sunlight coming into the garden, and not landing on the ground but higher up on a fence. If this is the case you can use raised planters, hanging planters or vertical gardens to access the sunlight and increase the range of vegetables and herbs that you can grow.

With partial shade your options are significantly improved. Many green, leafy vegetables including lettuce, spinach, kale, silverbeet and Asian greens like bok choy will do well with as little as 3 hours of sunlight a day. These have become the staples in my vegetable patch as the amount of shade has increased.

One of the useful things that you can do to maximise the sunlight that you do get in a shady garden is to paint the walls or fences with light reflective paint, which will reflect any available sun and warmth onto plants and encourage growth. This is also a useful trick for creating a microclimate for growing say a tropical or temperate plant such as a banana in a cool climate garden.

Another option that I have read about, but probably would not recommend, is to use mirrors. These can be used to reflect the sunlight into shaded areas, so that you can make better use of this space.

However, this is not an ideal solution as the mirror doesn't reflect all the sunlight in the same spectrum as direct sunlight. Also, the path of the sun varies throughout the year, so to make maximum use of this option you would have to be able to move the mirror using a sun-tracking device. However, this can be a choice if all other alternatives are not viable.

38. I'm renting! How can I take my vegetable garden with me when I move?

One of the really great things about growing your plants in pots and planters is that you can take it with you when you move.

When I rented at my last place before I moved to my current home, I grew my whole garden in pots! I had pots full of herbs, a pot of eggplants, two pots of tomatoes and a polystyrene box full of asparagus. That doesn't count the many pots I had for my non-edibles like roses and gardenias. It took nearly a full day just to move the garden!

So, if you are renting, don't let that stop you from trying to grow at least some of your own vegetables, herbs and even fruit. I know some landlords are pernickety about you leaving the property the same as you found it (Really?? Would they like me to go out and find a lot of dead cockroaches to replace the ones I had to clean out?).

I know that, as a tenant you don't want to start a garden and then leave your vegetables behind if you move, but there are some low-cost options that allow you to grow vegetables and herbs and fruit and take it with you when you move.

I have grown a citrus tree in a large plastic tub that I had drilled holes in the bottom for drainage, pawpaw and blueberries in large pots and asparagus in polystyrene boxes that were free from the local green grocer.

When it comes time to move the plants, I find it best to prepare the plant by giving them a weak seaweed solution a few days before the move, and then no water for a day or so immediately before the move. This will help reduce the weight of the pots, and make it easier to lift and carry them. You can give them a good drink when you get them to your new home.

It is generally a good idea to have a bit of a plan about where you want to locate the plants in your new home, so they can be placed directly in their new location. If you have been growing your vegetables in polystyrene boxes, I would recommend that you get new boxes as the polystyrene tends to break down after being watered and exposed to the sun, so they don't travel well. If you have been using them to grow perennial plants like asparagus or rhubarb, then you can dig these plants up and wrap them in damp newspaper until you get to your new home where you can either plant them in a new pot or plant them in the ground.

Chapter 7

ABOUT WATERING AND FERTILISING

This Chapter is about how to look after your vegetable and herb garden, and why you need to care for it.

Organic and inorganic fertilisers
Rohanne Young

39. *How do I water my vegetable garden?*

Without regular water plants die, and there is nothing more frustrating than putting a lot of effort into growing your own vegetables just to see them shrivel up and die on a hot day!

Whenever I establish a vegetable garden, the first thing I think about, after sun and location, is how I am going to water the plants. For small pots and planters, it is easy to use a watering can or the hose, but for larger garden beds I prefer to install an automated drip watering system.

A drip-type irrigation system is great as it delivers the water directly to the root zone of the plant, ensuring maximum uptake.

It also helps prevent plant diseases, like mould and mildew which can occur if the leaves of some plants get wet and don't dry properly. Overhead spraying is not recommended for vegetables as it can also help spread rust spores and other problems among plants. This is also true when spraying with water from a hose. You should aim the water at the base of the plant and not just water the leaves, otherwise the plants may still be thirsty even after you have spent several minutes watering them!

If possible, vegetables and herbs should be watered in the morning so that the plant can use the water during the day. I find that some days I don't have the time to spend each morning watering the vegetable patch by hand, so it is good to know that the vegetables have had some water from the drip system to keep them going throughout the day.

And when I do have time in the evening, it is not always recommended to water your vegetables, as some plants are not happy if they sit in wet soil overnight, especially when the night temperatures get cold or even freezing in winter. This is much less of an issue for plants in summer, when it can be common for your vegetables to need watering in the evening as well as in the morning.

I connect the drip system to an automatic timer so that the watering happens at the same time every day in summer or two to three days in winter. Automatic timers can be purchased at your local nursery or hardware store. They range from low-cost battery-operated units up to fully integrated electrical systems.

While I have previously put in the electrical systems I find that the battery-operated systems are more than adequate for your small suburban garden. When you have installed a battery operated timer, make sure that you check on the battery power on a regular basis. I have been caught a few times with a flat battery and a very dry garden!

40. *How often should I water?*

How often you water depends on what plants you are growing, what season it is and whether the plants are in pots or in the ground. I find that new plants, especially seedlings need to be watered every day until they are established, as they don't have a large enough root system to allow them to cope without water, even for a short period of time.

During periods of hot weather, or if it is windy, new plants may even need to be watered more than once a day. I also find that plants in pots and raised planters can dry out quickly in hot or windy weather, and may need to be watered twice daily in summer to stop the plants from drying out too much.

This is particularly so when you are looking at hanging pots. I grow several herbs and edible flowers in hanging pots and these can take a real beating on a hot day!

Too much water can also be deadly for the average plant. Plants are living things and, as such, they need to breathe, and not just through their leaves.

Their roots also need to be able to breathe and take up oxygen. If a plant's roots are stuck in water for too long it will drown.

A plant that has too much water will show similar warning signs as a plant that needs water. These signs include dull looking, wilting and droopy leaves.

Giving water at this point will often kill the plant, so before I give a drooping plant some water, I try to remember to check the soil around the roots to check that it is dry, not wet. I have forgotten to do this a couple of times and the poor plant has died.

Finally it is important to remember that just because it has rained, doesn't mean that your plants will have received enough water. You still need to keep watering your garden, or at least check to see that your plants did get enough water from the rain as, unless you have had steady rain, it may have barely made its way into the top few centimetres of the soil.

In the tropics and sub-tropics we can have torrential rain in summer, which can lead to the ground becoming waterlogged. During the most recent summer we struggled through about 8 months without any rain and then had almost a whole year's supply of rain in 3 weeks. Disappointingly my rosemary bush, which was about one and a half metres tall and the same in distance across, became waterlogged and drowned.

During torrential rain it is best to delay all hand watering, although spraying a weak liquid fertiliser or seaweed tonic, onto the leaves of your plant can really help your plants to survive.

41. *What about water crystals and soil wetters? Do they help?*

One of my favourite stories involved a client who, when asked how the drainage was in his garden replied "Awesome. The water just runs away!"

Like this gardener, you may find that no matter how often you water a garden bed it always seems dry and the plants always look wilted. Or you may have a plant in a pot where the water drains straight out of the drainage holes, so you think this means that the plant has enough water.

What it frequently means is that the soil has become hydrophobic. This happens when a waxy substance coats the soil particles and this repels the water rather than absorbing it.

To deal with this, gardeners often resort to soil wetting agents, which can be used to help the soil absorb water again. Commercial wetting agents are like a detergent and they change the way the soil and water interact. However, they can also interfere with the worms and microbes in the soil, affecting the longer-term health of your soil.

Another product intended to help improve the water holding capacity of soil are water-storage granules. These are small crystals that are designed to absorb up to four hundred times their weight in water and to hold the water in the soil for the plant to use.

This means that plants can go for longer without being watered, but they will eventually dry out and may, over time, become water resistant.

I prefer to use natural methods such as lots of compost and mulches, like sugar cane, as soils high in organic matter should not become water resistant or hydrophobic.

However, like everything, this isn't a set and forget solution. You have to keep topping up the organic material using compost, manures and mulches.

Seaweed contains natural wetting agents, so seaweed solution can be applied to your plants without harming them or adding any artificial wetting agents. By applying a weak seaweed solution to your plants fortnightly you should not need to add commercial wetting agents.

I have more of a problem with potting mix becoming hydrophobic over time with my potted plants. The water starts running straight through the pot and out the bottom, as soon as you apply it and you know that the plant can't be getting any. In these cases I generally repot the plant, adding fresh potting mix.

More commercial potting mixes are now being sold with the water storage gels or crystals included.

So, are water crystals necessary or helpful? I prefer to use home-made compost, coir peat or coconut fibre as they help retain water naturally. I mix coir peat into the potting mix when potting up new plants into containers, as it not only helps with water retention, it also helps make the pots lighter. And should you overwater your plants or have a deluge of summer rain, they will allow this to drain away naturally so your plants don't drown!

Also you need to be careful as some of the really cheap water crystals actually contain polyacrylamide which is the substance used in disposable nappies. While this is great for absorbing water it isn't so great at releasing the water when your plants need it. So, if you do want to use water crystals, aim for an acrylamide-free product.

42. How do I fertilise my plants?

Like all living things plants need food to survive and grow. The important thing to remember with plants is that they are "captive" beings. This means that when they are hungry they cannot go out and seek food like humans can.

Conversely, if you overfeed a plant it cannot get away from this excess, which can actually harm it. That is why I do not use inorganic fertilisers, but more about that soon.

There are two main ways that you can feed your plants, through the leaves as a foliar feed, and by improving the soil quality adding composts and natural foods.

When I was first learning about fertiliser I was told all about the importance of the N-K-P concentrations. All plants require three main nutrients to survive and thrive. These are nitrogen (N), phosphorous (P) and potassium (K) or potash.

Fertilisers that contain all three nutrients, N-K-P are considered complete fertilisers, although the actual concentrations of each nutrient can vary significantly.

This often has more to do with different manufacturers and different concentrations than actual plant needs. For example a fertiliser with an NPK of 10-10-10 contains twice as much fertiliser by weight ratio than an NPK of 5-5-5.

When buying fertiliser for your plants you will notice more and more specialised fertilisers becoming available, such as "Herb and Vegetable" fertiliser or "Tomato" fertiliser, for specific types of vegetables.

You could fill the shelves of your garden shed with specialized fertilisers and I must admit that, early on in my vegetable growing journey I did go through a stage of buying "vegetable fertiliser", "herb fertiliser" and "tomato fertiliser". Then I realised that, if you read the fine-print, the NPK was the same and all the micronutrients were the same or very similar.

Now, to save myself both time and money, and to prevent my shelves from becoming crowded, I stick with one or two good general organic fertilisers, plus lots of homemade compost. This also makes it a lot easier when you are fertilising your garden as you can spread the same fertiliser around to many plants rather than making separate tasks to fertilise your tomato plants, then your lettuce and greens, and then your fruit trees.

Plants also require many minerals and other micronutrients; the same way we humans do. These can be divided into the macro-nutrients, which are calcium, sulphur and magnesium as well as a large number of micro-nutrients including iron, boron, manganese, copper, chloride, molybdenum and zinc.

If your soil is lacking any of these nutrients then your plants may not grow well and can show evidence of the deficiency. Where I am, in South East Queensland, the soils are naturally deficient in boron, so I make sure I give my plants enough boron to survive and thrive.

The macro-nutrients and micro-nutrients that plants need is important, not just so the plant thrives, but also because this is where we get most of our micronutrients from. To ensure the plants have all the micronutrients they need, you can supply them with a complete plant fertilizer or you can purchase many of the micronutrients separately, for situations where you may have a soil deficient in a particular micronutrient.

You will only know if your soil has a micronutrient deficiency if you have your soil properly tested by a laboratory, although some plants may exhibit signs that they are deficient in an essential nutrient. For example, in my garden silverbeet will develop brown stripes in the white stalk, which tells me that it is deficient in boron so I need to apply more boron to the soil.

Don't forget to also factor in the pH of the soil (refer Question 16), as all the minerals and micronutrients may actually be present in the soil, but the plant cannot access them because the pH is wrong.

43. *When and how often should I apply fertilizer?*

Vegetables and herbs are generally fast-growing plants and need regular food in order to grow well. When feeding a plant, you are actually feeding the soil. It's from the soil that the plant will access all its food requirements.

When I feed my soil, I use lots of mulch and compost. I draw up a schedule of when I need to fertilise each part of the garden so that I remember when to fertilise my plants. Otherwise you can think "Oh, I did that last week" when in reality it was several weeks or even months ago!

Some plants require more frequent feeding, so I spot feed and in my schedule I will note "fertilise citrus every second month on the first Tuesday". I find using an online calendar helpful, as it gives me a reminder when the tasks need doing. Other people use Apps, and there are some really useful Apps available for this.

The plants that are in pots and raised planters need more frequent feeding than the plants that are in the garden, as potted plants have their root zone restricted, and cannot search for nutrients from the surrounding area.

It is generally recommended that pot plants are fed with a small amount of slow release fertiliser every two months.

In summer I supplement this with an organic liquid fertiliser every two to three weeks, alternating with either a seaweed solution or worm tea. In winter I leave out the application of the slow release fertiliser, unless it is warm and the plants are still growing actively, but you should continue with liquid feeds unless your plants are totally dormant.

Generally, you should fertilise when your vegetables and herbs are growing vigorously. Applying fertiliser when the plant is not actively growing results in a waste of your fertiliser, time and money. It also can actually harm your plants and the surrounding soil, depending on the type of fertiliser used.

However, this doesn't mean you stop fertilising in winter, as many winter growing vegetables and herbs are actively growing in this period and still require food. When fertilising winter vegetables and herbs, I use organic liquid food instead of slow release pellets or granular fertilisers.

This is because lower soil temperatures can reduce the amount of fertiliser released into the soil for uptake by plants. However, liquid fertilisers are in a form that can be rapidly taken up by plants regardless of soil temperatures.

Your fertilising schedule should also consider the type of soil that you have. As my garden is mostly clay, which I have been slowly converting to loam soil, an application of a complete fertiliser twice a year is usually sufficient, especially when this is in the form of compost and added organic material and is supplemented with applications of organic liquid fertiliser during active growing periods.

However, if you are gardening on sandy soil, you will need to apply smaller amounts of slow-release fertiliser more regularly. This is because sandy soils lack the structure and density to retain nutrients in the plant's root zone.

When using a foliar feed I generally apply it in the early morning so that the plant can gain benefit during the day. In summer, when we can have torrential rain in the sub-tropics, I use a weak fertiliser or seaweed tonic as a foliar or leaf feed to ensure the plants have the nutrients they need to survive

The easiest way to do this is to mix fertiliser or seaweed solution in a spray bottle diluted with water and spray it on the leaves. The solution needs to look like weak tea. Any stronger and it can burn the plant.

44. There are lots of different fertilizers available. What is the difference between them?

When I first started growing my own vegetables and herbs I would go into my local garden centre and just be overwhelmed by the rows and rows of bagged, packaged and bottled fertilisers. It can seem like you need a science degree just to figure out which one to select. Do you need a different one for tomatoes versus herbs versus green leafy vegetables? It can seem that way if you read all the headings and product descriptions.

And when I first started, I did used to buy lots of different types of feriliser. And I would buy what was on special. And I didn't really care if it was organic or inorganic. Then slowly I started to realise that a lot of them had exactly the same NPK ratios, and the same micronutrient concentrations, so I became much more discerning.

Then I started learning more about soil health, and all the worms and microbes that were relying on me to make the best choice for their health as well as the health of my plants. So, if you are just starting to learn all this, or are still overwhelmed whenever you walk into the garden centre, here is a few of the things I have learnt.

Each fertiliser lists the various nutrients and their concentrations on the packaging or labels so you can know whether it is high or low in nitrogen, phosphorus and potassium. The higher the number, the more of that nutrient will be in the fertiliser. Generally, fertilisers sold as flower and fruit fertilisers contain lower levels of nitrogen and are higher in phosphorus and potassium than ordinary fertilisers.

Higher nitrogen levels will lead to lush green growth, but this may be at the expense of the flowers and fruit. This is great if you want to grow lettuce, kale, spinach and other green leafy vegetables. However, it's not so great if you want to grow pumpkins or tomatoes or eggplant.

Phosphorous stimulates good root growth and flower and fruit production, while the potassium helps the plant make sugars, as well as strengthening the plant walls. This is what you need if you want to grow plants that produce flowers and fruit.

The fertilisers can be divided into two main groups, those that are manufactured or man-made and those derived from natural sources.

Within these two groups you will find several subgroups including liquids, pellets and dry granules. Each has their own benefits and limitations.

Manufactured fertilisers

Manufactured fertilisers are generally called synthetic or inorganic fertilisers.

Often they are derived from products that have been mined, such as rock phosphate, which is then treated with acids and other substances to purify them and increase their availability to plants. They do not generally come from petroleum products, although you will find this stated in many blogs and on many websites.

Manufactured fertilisers are faster acting than organic fertilisers and can provide nutrients to plants quickly. These fertilisers are generally in a granular form and include Ammonium Nitrate, Ammonium Phosphate, Superphosphate, and Potassium Sulphate. They are sold as both dry granules to be applied to the soil and as liquid or powdered concentrates, which are diluted in water before application.

Many of the granular fertilisers are controlled-release fertilisers, where the fertiliser granules are coated with a layer that allows a bit of fertiliser to be released through the coating and into the soil each time water is applied.

However, because they are released each time water is applied, there is no "off" switch. The plant gets the nutrients whether it is actively growing or dormant.

This means that it becomes more important when you actually apply the fertiliser, and how much you apply. You need to be much more aware of seasonal and weather changes with inorganic fertilisers than you do with organic fertilisers as they can be leached out of your soil and into storm water drains meaning you plants don't get the benefits.

Manufactured fertilisers **must** be applied at the dosage rate and schedule recommended on the packaging, as an overdose of these fertilisers can kill your plants.

Organic fertilisers

Organic fertilisers are typically based on organic materials including blood and bone meal, poultry and cow manure, fish meal and seaweed emulsion. They are available in both pelletised and liquid forms. Organic fertilisers are slower acting than manufactured fertilisers, as instead of being activated by water, they are broken down by bacteria in the soil, providing nutrients to the plants as they decompose.

The bacteria are slower acting in winter, thereby naturally modifying the amount of nutrients made available to your plants. Because these fertilisers act slowly, it's almost impossible to kill your plants by applying too much.

Liquid organic fertilisers can be a quick way to give your plants a boost if applied to the soil, or diluted and applied as a foliar spray.

As organic fertilisers need to be broken down by microorganisms in the soil, they lead to an increase in these microorganisms, which is beneficial to both your plants and the soil. By adding organic fertilisers, along with other organic matter such as compost to your soil, over time you will change the soil structure to a rich, loamy crumb-like structure. This will improve the water retention capabilities of your soil and enhance soil fertility.

Seaweed-based fertilisers are a popular form of organic fertiliser, although many seaweed solutions do not contain high enough NKP ratios to be considered complete fertilisers. This can be resolved by the addition of fish emulsion to the seaweed solution.

These fertilisers provide nutrients that are immediately available to plants. They also contain Mannitol, a compound that enhances absorption of any nutrients that are already present in the soil.

Seaweed fertilisers nourish the soil-dwelling bacteria that fix nitrogen in the soil and make it available to the plants. Applied as a diluted foliar spray, seaweed-containing fertilisers can have considerable impact, with plants producing new growth, and becoming greener in a matter of days.

45. Which is better: Manufactured or organic fertilizers?

In reality, if you are buying them in a bag at the nursery or garden centre they have all been "manufactured". The main differences between the two types of fertilisers comes down to whether the base product is a renewable resource or a finite resource and whether they support soil life.

Manufactured fertilisers are generally created from products that are mined, such as rock phosphates and these are a finite resource which, once depleted, cannot be replaced. Organic fertilisers are generally created from the by-products of living animals, including chicken and cow manure and blood and bone, so are considered a renewable resource.

Both manufactured and organic fertilisers can provide your plants with nitrogen, phosphorous and potassium, so once they are applied to your plants in the correct dosage, plants cannot distinguish between an organic fertiliser and a manufactured fertiliser, as the nutrients are processed in exactly the same way.

Although manufactured fertilisers give your plants access to nutrients quickly, they don't add any organic matter or micronutrients to the soil. This means that they do not support the microbiological life in the soil, and can actually harm earthworms and soil microbes if applied incorrectly.

Organic fertilisers on the other hand, actually require the microorganisms in the soil to break them down and make the nutrients available to the plants.

This results in an increase in beneficial microorganisms in the soil, which will improve your soil over time.

If only manufactured fertilisers are used, the soil will eventually become depleted of organic matter, and you will need more and more fertiliser to achieve the same level of growth in your plants.

I now only use organic fertilisers, as I have come to appreciate how much better they are for my garden. I love it when I dig in the soil to plant vegetables and find great big fat earthworms as I know they are working with me, helping to break down organic material and to aerate the soil so that my plants grow strong and vigorous.

Chapter 8

COMPOSTING TO REDUCE WASTE

This Chapter is about how you can decrease your personal environmental impact through your edible garden.

Composting worms in my worm farm
Rohanne Young

46. How do I start composting?

It took me a long time to really embrace the whole concept of composting.

I didn't grow up in a household where composting of kitchen scraps was the norm. In fact, when I got my first garden after I left home, the gardener I shared with my neighbour wanted to build me a compost bin and I thought he was all sorts of crazy! Several decades and a lot of gardening and a lot more knowledge later, I wish I had listened and learnt more.

At the time Bob, the gardener, wanted to build me a 3 bay cold composting system. As he mowed the lawns and did all the pruning of trees and shrubs, he was even happy to do all the work involved in turning the compost heap regularly so that it produced great compost. Bargain!

What I have learnt since is that there are two main types of composting, hot composting and cold composting. Most people who compost know about, and use, the cold composting method.

I will explain the difference between the two systems as well as the advantages and disadvantages of both systems of composting.

Cold composting

Cold composting is a process where compost worms and microbes break down garden and kitchen waste material to create a rich food for your garden. This composting happens over a period of several months and can be continually added to, as kitchen and household scraps are generated. It can be carried out in small gardens and can take up only a small amount of space.

Apart from an optional weekly turn using a garden fork or a composting aerator, it is relatively free of physical exertion. If you decide to add air into your compost heap using a composting aerator, it will significantly speed up the process and provide you with composted hummus more quickly.

The main advantages to cold composting is that it is simple, it takes up a lot less space than a hot compost, it can be constantly added to as kitchen and garden waste are generated, it takes minimal effort and can be done at any time of the year, it is flexible and everyone can do it! Best of all it reduces the amount of waste that you send to landfill!

The main disadvantages of cold composting are that it can take several months to break down and give you the lovely rich loamy compost, it can look unsightly, it can attract pests and vermin and the amount of compost generated is considerably less than the amount of green and brown material that you have added to the compost heap over time.

During cold composting the volume of the original green and brown material can shrink by as much as 50 percent of the original volume.

Cold composting also does not generate enough heat to kill any weed seeds or pests and diseases that may be present. This means that you cannot add any weeds or plants that have gone to seed or any diseased plant material to your compost bin.

Hot composting

On the other hand, hot composting, as its name suggests, involves using heat and microorganisms to break the down the plant material. With a hot compost, you create the compost heap all in one go. This means you need to collect all the waste material that you want to compost together into a large pile.

This material includes green waste like grass clippings from the mower, leaves and small branches and kitchen scraps like vegetable peelings and coffee grounds. It also includes brown waste such as dried leaves, straw or sugar cane mulch, paper and other matter that can add carbon to the mix. There should be around 3 times more brown material than green material in order to make a nice balanced compost. This is because the brown material is a lot less nutrient dense than the green material.

The pile needs to be away from grass or plants that you wish to keep, as the temperatures get very hot and any surrounding plants can be killed. The compost heap is left for several days to allow the heat to build up, and then it can be turned manually every two to three days to speed up the process and ensure even decomposition of materials.

There are several advantages to hot composting, not least being that the whole process can be completed in as little as 18 days and it can create a large amount of compost for your garden. Because all the materials are collected and used immediately there is no chance of attracting pests and vermin. The hot composting process also kills any weed seeds and many pests or diseases that may be present in the plant material.

The main disadvantage is that you require quite a large garden to be able to build a hot compost heap. It can also be quite a manual task, requiring time and effort to turn the compost regularly.

47. Do I need to buy a compost bin to start composting?

After I moved away from Bob the gardener, I didn't do any composting for a long time. Then, when I moved to Brisbane, one of my friends was moving house and gifted me their old compost bin as they were moving to a much smaller block. So, I started collecting lawn clippings and composting vegetable and kitchen scraps and one day, when I didn't have enough potting mix, I used this compost that I had made and I was hooked!

So, if you are like I was, and have yet to discover the joys of composting, it really is easy. You don't actually need a compost bin to make compost, but you might want to use a bin to keep things looking a bit tidier.

There are several different types of compost bins commercially available including aerating bins, solid bins, worm tubes and tumbler bins. The other option is that you can make your own compost bays, like Bob built for me.

A home-made compost bin can be as easy as recycling an old plastic garbage bin or paint bucket and some composting worms. You may choose to remove the base and partially bury the bin or bucket in the ground so that soil microbes can enter the composting material and help speed up the process.

You can also build compost bins out of chicken wire or build wooden crates or boxes. I prefer to use the aerating bins, as they have a hatch at the base of the bin where the finished compost can be retrieved, without me having to empty the entire bin.

If you live on a small block or in a townhouse you may prefer to use one of the plastic compost bins without a hatch that has a tight-fitting lid as these can look nicer, as well as helping to keep out unwanted animals such as cockroaches and rodents.

48. I don't have much space. Can I do any composting?

Composting is one of those areas where there have been huge improvements, which means that you can compost your vegetable scraps and kitchen waste even if you only have a tiny amount of space. There are plenty of indoor compost bins, known as Indoor composters or Bokashi bins, and these are a great alternative for small yards and units.

If I didn't already have several compost bins, plus a worm farm, worm tubes and chickens I would love to have an Indoor composter, as then I wouldn't have to walk all my kitchen scraps out to the compost bin every evening!

The Indoor composter or Bokashi bin is basically a bucket with lid and tap which you place on, or under, your kitchen sink. You place any food scraps and peelings from your food preparation in the bin and when you've completed your food preparation, you cover the scraps with a compost accelerator. By covering the food scraps with the compost accelerator and having a lid, the bins don't smell and should not attract vermin or insects.

The compost accelerator contains bacteria, which helps the food to break down. When the bin is full, and the mix has decomposed, it can be buried in the garden where it will feed your plants. Don't be tempted to use the decomposed mix directly on your potted plants, as it is too concentrated and will burn or even kill your pot plants.

If you live in a unit or retirement unit and don't have access to any garden space, you can offer the contents of your Indoor composter bin to your body corporate or to your local community garden. They will generally be grateful to receive this composted material!

Another great option for home composting are worm farms, especially if you live in a townhouse or a small block that has some space available. Worm farms take up very little space and can be either single level or several tiers high, which allows for some material to be composting, while you are adding kitchen scraps to the newer layers.

A healthy worm farm should not smell. If your worm farm is smelling then it is out-of-balance, and the kitchen scraps are fermenting not composting. If this happens then you will need to slow down the amount of food you are giving to your worms until they can produce enough new worms to help eat up all the scraps.

A productive worm farm should easily compost all the kitchen scraps from a two-person household each week. If you want to start a worm farm you can buy complete, ready to assemble kits that contain everything you need, including the composting worms.

Worm farms won't give you a huge amount of compost or hummus to use in your garden, but they will produce a good quantity of worm tea. The worm tea is excellent for feeding your edible plants. Just dilute the concentrated tea by about 10:1 with water. It should look like a weak cup of tea, hence the name. Water it onto your plants, and onto the soil around your plants, as this will add more beneficial bacteria, as well as nutrients to the soil.

The worm juice needs to be drained off from the worm farm or else the hummus in the worm farm can become too wet for the worms. You will know if the worm farm is getting too wet as the worms will be climbing up the sides and trying to escape. Similarly, if your worm farm becomes too dry, you will often find it invaded by cockroaches or ants.

49. What can be composted?

It took me a little while to get to grips with the whole composting process. At first I was just adding kitchen scraps and lawn clippings and the compost bin got a bit slimy and sludgy and started to smell. Then I learnt that I needed to add both green and brown materials to my compost bin to get a balanced end-product and for it not to smell or be slimy.

Green materials include most fruit and vegetable peelings from your kitchen, vegetables languishing at the bottom of the fridge that are past their use-by date and have gone limp or mouldy, coffee grounds and teabags, and many other things that you might have previously thrown in the rubbish bin. I also add the dog fur and contents from the vacuum cleaner to the compost bin as, being organic, these break down into compost as well.

Other green material to add to your compost can include weeds from your garden or vegetable patch, as long as they haven't yet gone to seed, as well as trimmings and pruning's from your plants, and grass clippings from mowing the lawn. In fact, once you start looking around you will be amazed at what you can compost and how much your council waste is reduced as a result!

If you want your compost to break down quickly then you need to cut any plant stalks and large leaves into smaller pieces. This can be achieved easily by running over them with the mower.

There are also some plants that you definitely want to ensure are added to your compost. These are generally plants that have long tap roots, such as dandelions, as they grow down deep into the soil and take up vital nutrients that they store in their leaves and roots. Other plants such as Comfrey have become known as compost accelerators because of their positive impact on the composting process, both in terms of speeding up the process as well as adding micronurients to the compost.

A lot of blogs will tell you not to add onion skins or citrus peel to the compost, as the worms don't like these. However, I have not had any problems adding these to the bin, provided they are in small quantities. Many people encourage adding eggshells to the compost bin to improve the calcium content of your compost. I found that, unless I crushed the shells up, I had beautiful intact eggshells among my finished compost.

Among the brown material you can add to your compost are dried leaves, straw, sugar cane mulch, plant stalks, animal manures like cow and sheep poo as well as newspaper, shredded paper and cardboard.

When using cardboard boxes, it is best to remove any labels and sticky tape from the boxes before adding them to the compost, as these don't break down and you end up having to pull these from your completed compost before adding it to your garden. I have found this out the hard way!

As I found, if you add too much green material, and don't add enough brown material, your compost bin can become unbalanced and start to ferment. When the compost bin material ferments, this is when compost bins start to smell unpleasant.

Often the first sign that your compost bin is out-of-balance will be the presence of tiny little gnat-like flies. These are known as vinegar flies and can seem to appear out of nowhere. If you notice vinegar flies, then your compost heap is too acidic.

To correct this you need to add one to two handfuls of garden lime to decrease the acidity, and then you need to increase the level of brown material you are adding to your compost bin. This can be done easily by adding some straw, newspaper, dried leaves, shredded paper or cardboard to the compost bin.

My compost bins are much better balanced since I started adding the straw and chook poo from my weekly clean out of the chook house!

50. What can't be composted?

There are a few materials that I never add to my compost bin. These include any meat, dairy or animal products, as they can attract rodents and snakes to your compost, even if you have a sealed system with a tight-fitting lid. They also smell as they decompose, which reinforces the idea many people have that composting is a smelly business.

Not adding these things to your compost bin actually makes sense, as you wouldn't normally leave prawn heads or old meat or similar produce laying around outside, as you know it would go off and attract flies and smell bad. The compost bin is no different! A balanced compost bin should never smell unpleasant.

Also, although you can add newspaper to your compost it is not recommended you add the printed brochures that come with newspapers or junk mail from your letter box, as they may contain a plastic coating which you don't want in your finished compost. There is also some question about some of the inks that are used in the printing and whether these may be harmful.

When adding lawn clippings to my compost, I make sure that I don't add any grass or weed seeds. This means a bit more work, especially in summer as I have to mow my lawn more frequently before it starts to flower and produce seeds.

Although I don't use them, if you have treated your lawn with any weed and feed product, or sprayed for Bindi or other weeds, then you cannot add the lawn clippings to your compost until this product is no longer present. This can mean that you cannot compost your lawn clipping for several weeks or even months.

Otherwise your lovely homemade compost could actually end up killing your plants, as most of these chemicals are residual and will kill most broad leaf plants! In fact, these chemicals aren't broken down in either a cold compost system or a hot compost system.

I don't add dog poop to my compost bin, as my dogs have a primarily meat-based diet, and so their poop does not compost well. Also, you may be adding harmful bacteria to your soil, which is not a good idea especially if you want to use the compost for your vegetables and herbs.

However, I have purchased a special dog poop compost bin, which I have buried in the ground and place the dog poop down into this compost tube. I cover each layer with a bit of sawdust to make sure that the smell doesn't knock me out when I add more poop to the tube. Worms and microbes break down the poop, which saves it from going to the rubbish tip and landfill.

Other materials that you shouldn't put in your cold compost include the flower heads of weeds, or any plant that has gone to seed or developed fruit. Most compost bins do not get to a high enough temperature to kill these seeds, so you will later find them coming up in the gardens where you spread your compost.

This doesn't just apply to weeds. Many gardeners find that they have a great crop of cherry tomatoes, pawpaw or pumpkins growing from their compost. If you don't want this to happen you can either remove the seeds before composting, or pull the seedlings up like you would remove any other weed.

Likewise, with sick and diseased plants, I don't add them to the compost as you can end up spreading the disease to your healthy plants.

51. What are composting worms and how are these different from normal garden worms?

Like all children I was fascinated by worms, but after I left childhood behind I used to think worms were a bit icky. It wasn't until years later that I started to appreciate their role in the whole cycle of life.

When I first started I didn't know that there are around 3,000 different types of earthworms. Or that earthworms can range in size from as little as 0.5cm in length to

15cms or longer. All worms like to live in a moist environment where they have plenty of food, oxygen and the right temperatures, so you can understand their attraction to compost bins and worm farms.

I also didn't know that there were special types of worms used in composting. The most common are called the red wiggler worm, which is also known as the red worm, manure worm or tiger worm. And they really are quite red, not pinkie-brown like earthworms.

Red wiggler worms are small compared to other earthworms, generally growing to a maximum of 4 cm long, and they are not nearly as thick as earthworms. (And yes, their name is Red Wiggler. This is not a typo!)

In fact, they are generally not much thicker than a piece of straw, which makes it astounding when you see how much they eat! Red wigglers are also different to earthworms as they prefer to live near the top of the compost bin, where they feed on fresh plant material and scraps. This is what makes them ideal as composting worms.

I love opening up my worm farm to add kitchen scraps and seeing all the composting worms on the surface waiting for their next meal.

They will each eat up to their own weight in organic matter daily and, when conditions are suitable, they will breed rapidly, increasing in number so that they can process even more food. By eating large quantities of plant material and living near the surface, they can easily munch through the kitchen scraps that are added to the compost bin or worm farm each day. When they eat the plant material they digest it and leave behind worm castings, which provide plants with just the right nutrients in the form that they can easily access.

Normal earthworms also eat organic material, but they prefer to take the organic matter from the surface of the soil and carry it underground, where they prefer to live. While earthworms will also eat up to their body weight in food daily, they prefer to dwell deep in the soil, so are not nearly as useful in a compost bin as the Red Wigglers.

Earthworms are better at improving general soil quality. They do this by burrowing deep into the soil and breaking up the soil, which allows oxygen and water to filter down deeper. Earthworms also leave behind their castings, which provide nutrients for plants. Earthworms are ideal for outdoor gardens and are often found in your vegetable garden and in flower beds.

Composting worms aren't usually found in your backyard, so they need to be bought in when you start a compost bin or worm farm. Red wiggler composting worms can be purchased from most nurseries or hardware stores that sell worm farms or compost bins. Otherwise you can get some compost worms from anyone you know who already has a worm farm or compost bin. Because of the rate at which they reproduce, most gardeners are happy to share some of their compost worms with someone who is just setting up a worm farm or compost bin.

52. Help, I have maggots and cockroaches in my compost bin! What am I doing wrong?

A lot of people get really concerned when they first start composting and they see maggots or cockroaches in their compost bin. However, this is perfectly normal and even healthy!

It takes a lot of critters to break down the organic matter in your compost bin to create compost. And these do include maggots! Before you get totally grossed out, you need to realise that these maggots are the pupae of the saw fly, which is one of the beneficial insects. They are not the maggots of house flies.

I too got a bit grossed out when I first saw these maggots in my compost bin! Once I found out that they were just as important in creating compost as the composting worms, I managed to deal with them better!

What you don't want in your compost bin are rats and mice or ants, or even too many cockroaches.

If you have a lot of cockroaches in your compost bin, or if it is overrun with ants, then your compost is too dry. This means that apart from the insects, it also won't decompose to create compost. You need to provide some water to your compost heap to help it break down and create the compost.

The compost should be damp but not wet, otherwise you will drown the worms and bacteria and your compost will start to smell! To test the dampness, get a handful of compost and squeeze it. It should hold together into a loose ball. Not fall apart into crumbs or hold together like mud.

53. Good bacteria? Is there such a thing?

I was brought up to believe all bacteria are bad and will cause us harm. You had to wash your hands to get rid of germs, make sure you only ate fresh food because if it was even slightly off you could get food poisoning and you had to keep your house clean to make sure that germs and bacteria couldn't survive.

It took me a long time to realise that the majority of bacteria are not only good, some of them are essential for us to be able to live and to grow our food. This doesn't mean that you shouldn't wash your hands or make sure that you don't eat food that is suspect, just that bacteria can also be beneficial to you and the environment.

Healthy soil is alive with a whole world of different microorganisms including bacteria and fungi. These organisms are fundamental to the health of the soil, and to the life of plants growing in the soil, as they help break down leaves, manures and other organic matter to make the nutrients available to plants. These microorganisms are the same ones that help break down the organic material in your compost bin and turn it into rich compost.

When you add the freshly made compost to your soil, you also add all these good bacteria to your soil. This is one of the reasons that compost is so good for your garden.

Bacteria have a number of important roles in the soil. Some of them extract nitrogen from the air and turn it into a form that can be used by plants. As I discussed in Question 43 all plants require nitrogen as an essential macronutrient. Although nitrogen makes up around 80 percent of the air, it is not naturally part of soil, so microorganisms have evolved to convert the atmospheric nitrogen into a form that can be available to plants.

Scientists are now discovering that some of the microorganisms, including mycorrhizal fungi also live in and among the roots of plants and help them to convert other nutrients, including the minerals that plants need, into a form that is useable by the plant. Current research is showing that these fungi can actively search out nutrients for plants and bring them to the roots of a plant, so the plant can access essential nutrients that are not in its immediate growing zone.

Other microorganisms are beneficial in controlling the bad bacteria, known as pathogens, in the soil so they help to keep your plants healthy. Along with worms, soil bacteria also help the soil to breathe.

I remember once ripping up some black plastic that had been laid under a garden bed and nearly being knocked over by the sour vinegary smell. I have never used black plastic in a garden since then, as I learnt that this meant that all the beneficial microorganisms had died and the soil was effectively dead as well. It took a lot of work to make that garden productive and healthy.

Chapter 9

WEEDS AND OTHER PLANTS YOU DON'T WANT

This Chapter is about the plants you don't want and how to deal with them.

Oxalis weed in my garden
Rohanne Young

54. What are weeds?

When I first started writing this book, which admittedly was some time ago, I had a large chapter on weeds. They were the bane of my existence, or so I thought!

Since then I have learnt much. I have learnt that weeds are often telling us what our soils are deficient in, and whether our soil is acidic or alkaline. When we address the mineral deficiencies and the pH problems, the weed problem mostly disappears!

And while I always knew that weeds, by their very definition, are just plants that are growing where you don't want them to grow, I have also learned that many plants that are considered weeds are actually edible! Not only edible, some taste really good.

And they often contain more health-giving nutrients than many of the plants that we grow as food. A lot of the plants that we grow as food in Australia are not indigenous to our country. This means that they were originally imported into Australia and some, such as fennel, lemongrass and asparagus have become weeds in our native bushlands. Similar problems are encountered in many other countries.

Many new gardeners, and even long term gardeners starting over, find that when you first start to prepare your vegetable garden prior to planting, your soil is suddenly covered in weeds. Where did these weeds come from? You know you didn't plant them!

Often the seeds of these plants have been lying dormant in your soil for a long time and they take full advantage of your hard work, your compost and fertiliser to set themselves up in your vegetable and herb garden. Once there, they can out-compete your freshly planted crops for both water and nutrients, developing a stronger root system than your carefully nurtured vegetables.

You can aim for a weed-free garden, although sometimes it is more beneficial to do some research and find out whether these weeds can be repurposed into food. For example, I used to curse the weed Purslane, until I learnt that you can eat it. It actually tastes like cucumber and is really good in salads. It can also be used in pesto-style sauces and my chickens absolutely love it. On top of that it is an excellent plant-based source of omega3 fatty acids, which are essential for our health. Since I discovered its many uses, I have trouble growing it! Ironic huh.

If you do decide that you need to remove the weeds, it is often easier to find out what the weed is telling you about your soil and then changing the soil profile. For example, nutgrass prefers to grow in acidic soils that are deficient in calcium and other micronutrients. I have found that by addressing the deficiencies, the nutgrass problem is significantly reduced.

55. *Why do I need to remove weeds?*

There are some weeds, like Oxalis and Singapore daisy, that really are a nuisance. These are the weeds that I try and control through manual weeding, steaming and poisoning. When I do use poison I only use organic, non-toxic poisons as I don't want to introduce toxic chemicals into my soil or my vegetable garden.

Bear in mind that you are planning on eating the crops you grow in the soil. So, if you use strong chemicals they can be absorbed by your vegetables, herbs and fruit, and you may end up introducing these poisons into your diet. To my way of thinking this somewhat defeats the purpose of growing healthy food that is good for you!

Most plants that have become weeds have done so because of their ability to grow and reproduce rapidly.

These plants can generate large numbers of seeds, often in rapid succession. These seeds are then wind-borne or transmitted by native animals such as birds, who eat the seeds and transport them to new sites in their droppings. Humans also help transmit the seeds on our clothes and footwear.

When planting your vegetables and herbs, it is important to ensure that you do not inadvertently create a weed problem by allowing your plants to set seed. Fennel, dill, lemongrass and asparagus are all examples of vegetable and herb plants that have escaped from the domestic garden and become environmental weeds in the Australian bushland. These plants can also become weeds in other parts of your own garden, growing in the grass or in other garden beds.

I learnt this lesson the hard way when I let some lemongrass go to seed. It took me a long time to get rid of the lemongrass seedlings that came up in gravel pathways, in cracks in the drive and throughout the lawn.

56. How do I get rid of weeds?

When I was little I remember my dad talking about my grandfather and questioning the fact that my grandfather would dig up weeds and just leave them on top of the garden bed. Dad thought this was being lazy, as surely the weeds would just continue growing? I have since learnt that my grandfather actually knew what he was doing, as this "solarised" the weeds, which killed them but left them to break down and return their nutrients to the soil!

This was in the days before wide scale herbicides were available, and the traditional method of weed removal was to dig the weeds out by hand, or to use a hoe to cut the weed off at ground level before it flowered or set seed.

In some ways we have come a long way since those days. There are lots of chemicals available to poison weeds without you having to put in all that manual effort. However, most of these contain the chemical Glyphosate. The problem with spraying your weeds with chemicals is that you have to be really accurate, as the chemicals don't discriminate between the weeds you want to get rid of, and the vegetables and herbs that you want to keep healthy. They will kill both wanted plants and unwanted plants equally.

Another problem with Glyphosate-based weedkillers is that they have been found to be potential carcinogens, which means they can cause cancer! This means when using these poisons you must wear gloves and a face mask to ensure none of the chemical gets on your skin and so you don't breathe in mist or fumes. Apart from not being good for you, Glyphosate-based weedkillers are not good for your pets or for the environment, with research showing that they can harm native frogs and disorient the bees in your garden!

Research is also proving that, despite claims to the contrary, these chemicals can remain in the soil and be taken up in the plants you are growing! If you want to garden organically, that is without herbicides, then you will need to remove weeds by hand.

As long as you make regular visits to your garden to pick your vegetables and herbs, you can remove any weeds and deal with any bugs at the same time. By having your vegetable and herb garden in a position where you visit it regularly, you can ensure that you pull out or dig up the weeds as they appear.

If any weeds escape your notice and do go to seed, and this can happen to the best of us, make sure that you remove any flowers and seed heads. Do not add these to your compost as this will encourage the development of further weeds in your garden. To dispose of weed seeds effectively place the seeds inside a plastic bag which can be securely tied and baked in the hot sun for several days to kill the weeds. I find old Ziploc bags really effective for this.

57. Is there an organic (healthy) way of killing weeds?

When I was between chickens, the chookyard became overgrown with weeds and I used to curse the fact that I had yet another weeding job to do! The soil was rock hard and the weeds had strong root systems. You also might find this when you are starting a new garden, or have been absent or busy for a while. Weeds have taken over everything in a short amount of time, and to hand weed feels like a massive amount of work, so it may seem like you have to resort to one of the Glyphosate-based weed killers.

Before you reach for the spray pack, there are actually a few friendlier ways of killing weeds in the garden that are not based on Glyphosate. A relatively new commercial product is based on Nonanoic acid or Pelargonic acid, which occurs naturally in plants including geraniums and pelargoniums.

This weedkiller works by removing the natural wax coating of a plant's leaves causing the plant to rapidly dry out and shrivel up. Like most weedkillers it is non-selective, so it will kill any plant it is sprayed on, so you still have to worry about spray drift. However, it doesn't travel through the soil so will have a limited effect on nearby plants.

A simple homemade weed killer can be made by mixing together 1 litre of cleaning vinegar, half a cup of salt and a splodge of dishwashing liquid. Mix everything together in a spray bottle, shake well until the salt has been dissolved into the vinegar. This weed killer works well on most weeds, even the dreaded wandering jew (tradescantia) and oxalis, but like most weed killers, it doesn't have any impact on nutgrass.

Make sure that you spray it directly on the weeds and avoid the soil as much as possible, as it is alleged that the salt can build up in the soil and make it difficult for your plants to grow later. I haven't found this to be the case and have been using this weedkiller for several years. I regularly check the pH of the soil and it doesn't appear to have had an effect.

Like most weed killers it isn't selective, meaning it will kill anything, so don't spray it on plants you want to keep! Also, don't spray it where you want to plant something straight away as the salt may interfere with new plant growth, and vinegar can temporarily affect the pH of the soil.

Don't use industrial vinegars as these are much higher in ascetic acid and can be harmful to you and the environment.

For nutgrass, I have found the application of sugar crystals to be an effective killer and so far the nutgrass has not returned! With other weeds, especially when I have only a few weeds to kill, I use plain boiling water poured straight on the centre of the weeds. Two or three applications of boiling water usually kills all but the toughest weeds. A household steam cleaner is also effective for this purpose.

58. *There are lots of chemicals at the nursery/hardware store. Do I need all of these?*

If you have read this far in the book you will probably have realised by now that I don't use many chemicals in my garden. This doesn't mean that you can't, and I have tried to provide you with enough information to make you own decisions.

When you go to your local nursery, garden centre or hardware store you will find rows and rows of chemicals. These chemicals include fertilisers, pesticides, weedkillers, minerals and trace elements and various other substances designed to feed or promote the growth of your plants and kill pests and weeds.

In my opinion many of these chemicals are expensive, unnecessary and often do not do what they claim. They all require more than one application to be effective. Also, pesticides and weedkillers are generally indiscriminate, meaning they will kill the good and the bad equally. This means they will kill the beneficial insects and your prized edible plants just as effectively as they will kill the bugs and weeds you are trying to destroy.

By destroying beneficial insects like bees, you are removing the insects that will actually pollinate your plants and ensure that you get a good supply of tomatoes, peas, beans or whatever fruit or vegetable you have planted. You are also destroying the good bugs that will help control the bad bugs in your garden. Sadly, the bad bugs often recover quicker, so you may be doing even more harm to your garden in the long term.

When using chemicals to control pests and diseases you need to be certain that you have identified the correct pest or disease. Spraying the wrong chemical not only wastes your time and money, it can actually have a negative effect on your plants and on the environment, as well as helping to increase future pest resistance.

In addition to this, many of these chemicals are not without risk to you, your family and your pets. Several of the chemicals designed to kill weeds and bugs do so by altering the growth and development blueprint of the plant or insect. Although they have undergone scientific testing on the weeds and bugs, there isn't yet long-term knowledge about what exposure to these chemicals can mean to human health.

This is why you will find directions on the chemicals label that require you to cover your skin with gloves and long sleeves, wear a face mask and not inhale any of the mist or fumes.

You will also find that there is generally a withholding period of several days or even weeks after spraying. What this means is that any foods sprayed with these chemicals cannot safely be eaten until this withholding period is over.

As I like to be able to eat my produce while I walk around the garden, eating peas or tomatoes or lettuce straight from the plant, I prefer to use one of the organic ways of controlling pests and diseases and removing weeds, without having to resort to chemical control.

Another problem with chemical pesticides is that more and more bugs and diseases are becoming resistant to the chemicals that were once effective in killing them, meaning that it will become harder to control outbreaks of these pests in the future.

Some of the pesticides such as pyrethrums, say they are natural as they come from plants or are made identical to natural substances. This does not automatically mean that they are safe for humans, especially when they are concentrated significantly beyond what they would be in nature, so you still need to take precautions when using these as a spray.

Organic pesticides include Eco Pest oils, Neem oil, Bacillus thuringiensis and actinobacteria and insecticidal soaps. Organic sprays can also cause problems if used incorrectly or at the wrong times. Many of these insecticides work on smothering the pest, so they can be just as deadly if sprayed on beneficial insects as on the bugs you want to get rid of.

There are some basic rules that you must comply with, when using any pest or weed sprays:

- Do not spray any pesticides, either organic or chemical on beneficial insects or when beneficial insects are feeding, which is often first thing in the morning;
- Make sure you only spray the affected plant(s) and avoid spray drift where possible;
- Do not spray your plants in the middle of the day;
- Only spray in calm weather when there is no wind; and
- Do not spray when your plants are stressed, as the oils can block the pores in the leaves and kill the plant.

Chapter 10

GOOD BUGS AND BAD BUGS

This Chapter is about how to deal with bugs and diseases in your vegetable garden - both the good guys and the gatecrashers.

One of the Good Guys: A Praying Mantis in my garden
Rohanne Young

59. What bug is eating my plants and how do I get rid of it?

When I first started trying to grow my own herbs and vegetables I became aware of a whole world of bugs that just seemed to appear from nowhere and eat all my lettuce, or kale, or broccoli just when I was about to harvest them! It was, and still is, incredibly frustrating!

Up until then I admit that I was a bit oblivious to the miriad of life forms that exist in a normal garden. And when I did start to become aware of this "alternate universe" I focussed first on the bad bugs or "pests".

Some of the "pest" bugs that can be present in your garden damage your plants by eating new growth, sucking the sap and possibly even injecting toxins into your plants. Some common pest bugs that are going to be eating your vegetables and herbs include aphids, caterpillars, grasshoppers, scale, mealybug and mites.

At first, like many gardeners, I used to spray chemicals to kill these unwanted and destructive pests. Most times I would also observe the mandated withholding periods. That was until someone introduced me to the world of good bugs! Wise mother nature has ensured that there is a predator for every pest likely to show up in your garden.

However, there is a little bit of a time delay between first seeing the pest, and one of its predators showing up. This makes sense as, before the pest showed up, the predator had no food supply.

This means that you should not aim for a bug free garden! If you totally eliminate the bad bugs from your garden, this will also do away with all the good guys, and your garden will be out of balance with nature. When a garden is out of balance it is even more vulnerable to attack by bad bugs.

A note regarding the treatment of many pest attacks. You will see the suggestion to apply a strong jet of water to wash the bugs off your plant. I used to think this was a silly recommendation. Surely it would just spread the pests to other nearby plants, and wouldn't they just come back anyway? That was until I found out that many of these pests can't actually move far by themselves. They need ants or other insects to help "farm" them, that is, to move them around.

The ants have developed a beneficial relationship with bugs like aphids, scale and mealybug. The ants pick them up and move the pest around the plant, and onto other nearby plants. In return the ants get to feed on the sugary substance, known as honeydew that the insects emit when they feed on plant sap.

So spraying with a strong jet of water does actually help disperse and control them! It can also temporaily remove or dilute some of the sugary solution, making the ants work harder for their food.

It is actually this honeydew, and the black sooty mould that grows on the honeydew that is often the first sign a gardener will have that their plants are being attacked. I often talk to gardeners who are seeking a fungicide to deal with the black sooty mould and tell them the pest that is really causing them problems.

Below I have described some of the many bad bugs that might show up in your garden, along with a description of the symptoms a plant will show when infected, and what you can do to control the problem as naturally as possible.

This list isn't meant to be exhaustive and is mostly comprised of those bugs that I have done battle with at some time in my own garden.

ANTS

Description: Ants on their own usually won't hurt your plants. The problem with ants is that they work with other pest bugs like mealybug or scale. The ants get to feed on the honeydew which is a sticky substance your plant produces when the bugs tap in and suck the sap. The only time ants can become a pest in their own right is if they create a nest in the roots of your potted plants which deprive the plant of soil and moisture

Ants
Rohanne Young

How to deal with them: The best way to deal with ants is to eliminate the scale and/or mealybug that the ants are farming. See the relevant bug that is on your plant for how to achieve this. Many gardeners have tried making barriers that the ants won't cross with Vaseline or similar. I find this can create other problems. I am having a fair amount of success with diatomaceous earth as a barrier. This looks like a dust but has very sharp microscopic edges that scratch the bodies of the ants when they try and cross it, leading to their dehydration and death.

APHIDS

Description: Aphids are bugs that suck the sap out of your plants, which will weaken your plant and can kill it. You know when you have aphids as lots of little green fly-like bugs will be seen around new growth. They often will fly off when you water the plants in the morning.

Aphids
in Ann Roffey's garden

How to deal with them: To deal with aphids, try hosing them off with a strong jet of water first thing in the morning. Encourage lacewing insects and lady beetles into your garden or buy in some lacewing or ladybeetle larvae. If you want to spray, try a homemade or commercial chilli, garlic and soap mix; Yates Success which is derived from beneficial soil bacteria; or Natrasoap, which is a potassium soap. Dilute as per instructions.

BROAD MITES

Description: Broad mites are so tiny they're impossible to see with the naked eye, hence the photo of affected leaves because this is what you will see. Broad mites act by injecting a toxic growth hormone into the plant, and this slows and distorts the plant's growth. Eventually, the leaves will turn yellow and die. Untreated, broad mites can kill your plant, as well as infecting other nearby plants, so treatment is an imperative.

Leaves showing broad mite distortion
Rohanne Young

How to deal with them: To treat broad mite, start by misting your plants with water regularly. This is best done late afternoon or evening in summer when the mites are most active. Mites hate being in a moist environment. Spraying the infected plant with Eco Oil will also help control broad mite as it smothers the mites. Make sure you spray both the top of the leaves and under the leaves and stems. Take care to use Eco Oil (not just pest oil) as Eco Oil contains a compound that attracts beneficial insects and lets them know that tasty snacks are available on a nearby plant!

CABBAGE MOTH/WHITE CABBAGE BUTTERFLY

Description: These are two of the main moths that you will see flying around your vegetable garden. They will lay their eggs on the leaves of your vegetables. They really like the Brassica family so will go for cabbages, broccoli and also lots of the Asian greens like bok choy. When the eggs hatch they become green caterpillars.

Cabbage Moth Butterfly
Rohanne Young

How to deal with them: The best ways I have found to eliminate the cabbage moth and white cabbage butterfly is to plant landcress. This is a plant which the cabbage moths and butterfly love and will lay its eggs in preference to any other plants. When the eggs hatch and the young caterpillars eat the leaves of the landcress it is extremely toxic and they die without completing their life cycle. The other thing that I have found effective is to make little white cabbage butterfly replicas out of plastic and attach these throughout your vegetable garden. Apparently, the cabbage butterfly is very territorial so it won't stay and lay its eggs in a garden it thinks is already infested.

CATERPILLARS

Description: Caterpillars are the larvae of moths and butterflies. You generally know if you have caterpillars as your plant will develop lots of holes in leaves, or the leaves may be totally eaten and you will usually see little black balls, which are the caterpillar's poop. Caterpillars have a ferocious appetite and can totally destroy your plants in a matter of hours.

Caterpillar
Rohanne Young

How to deal with them: I usually deal with caterpillars by picking them off and taking them around to my chickens. They love them! If you don't have chickens you can encourage wasps and micro-wasps into your garden, or buy in some micro-wasp larvae, as the wasps lay their eggs inside the caterpillar and eat them from the inside out. If you have paper wasps, make sure they don't nest in areas where people walk as you may get stung. If you want to spray caterpillars try a homemade chilli, garlic and soap spray. Dipel is an organic natural product based on Bacillus thuringiensis and is a great pesticide to use on caterpillars. Other natural products include Yates Success which is derived from beneficial soil bacteria and Yates Natrasoap which is a potassium soap. Neem oil is also an effective spray for caterpillars.

CITRUS LEAF MINER

Description: Citrus leaf miner are the young larvae of a tiny moth. The moth lays its eggs on new citrus leaves and the young offspring burrow into the leaves creating silver tracks across the leaf surface. In a bad infestation the leaves will become distorted and curled at the edges.

Citrus leaf miner trail
Rohanne Young

How to deal with them: Very few natural pesticides will kill citrus leaf miner. Spraying new citrus leaves with organic pest oil will deter the moth from landing and laying its eggs. Neem oil can also be an effective spray, as it penetrates the top layer of the leaves helping to destroy the leaf miner. Make sure that you pick off infected leaves and "bake" them in a plastic bag in the sun. This will prevent the larvae from hatching and reinfecting your plant. Do not compost infected leaves.

CITRUS GALL WASP

Description: Citrus galls are unsightly swellings on the stems of citrus trees, which are created as a result of irritation caused by the young larvae of the citrus gall wasp. The citrus galls, although unsightly will not kill your citrus tree, but may lead to fruit loss during a bad attack.

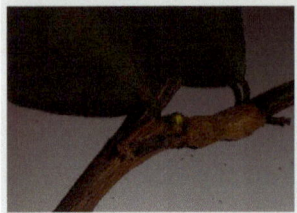
Citrus galls on lemon tree
Paul Boult

How to deal with them: Very few natural pesticides will kill the citrus gall wasp. The best way is to disrupt the life cycle. You can do this by removing the galls before the wasp has hatched. If you have too many to do this, you can slice through the gall with a razorblade. This opens the gall and kills the larvae. Just check that the larvae isn't ready to hatch as you might just be giving it an easy escape route. You can also try hanging bright yellow sticky traps in the branches of your citrus as these are supposed to trap the flying moth. I haven't tried this as I have a native beehive under my citrus and I don't want to trap my native bees by mistake

FRUIT FLY

Description: Depending on where you live in Australia, fruit fly can be a major problem in your vegetable garden. I have my biggest problem with fruit fly infecting my tropical nectarines and peaches but they can also cause major problems with tomatoes. The female fruit flies lay their eggs just under the surface of the fruit and the larvae, known as maggots eat their way through to the centre of the fruit, turning it into mush, or worse still, maggot infested. Fruit fly is not the same as vinegar flies that are those annoying little flies you get around fruit in the kitchen.

Fruit fly
Rohanne Young

How to deal with them: The best way to control fruit fly is through fruit fly traps. There are a number of traps available. Some traps use pheromones to attract the male fruit fly. If the males are destroyed then the females don't have eggs to lay so they won't infest your fruit. Other traps rely on baits such as wild may, Vegemite or proteins and they attract both the males and females. The wild may takes a year or two to be really effective as your garden has to go through a couple of life cycles of the fruit fly, which over-winters in the soil beneath the fruit trees. Free range chooks are also great at breaking the life cycle as they scratch up the soil around your fruit trees and eat the fruit fly larvae. If you have fruit fly, ensure that you collect and dispose of all infected fruit. You can also provide a physical barrier by enclosing your fruit in either cloth or paper bags. I have been using my vegetable bags that I use for buying my fruit and vegetables from the markets. These are made of recycled plastic and generally provide a good barrier to fruit fly.

GRASSHOPPERS

Description: Grasshoppers are a garden pest that will destroy all your plants, not just your vegetables. Grasshoppers have a ferocious appetite, and usually do most damage when they are small, and in their active growing phase. You will see them jump or fly off when you disturb any plants they are feeding on.

Grasshopper

How to deal with them: I deal with grasshoppers by trying to catch them and then feed them to my chooks. They go mad for them! However, if you don't have chooks try catching them in a net early in the morning when they are slower. A friend of mine cuts them in half with secateurs and brings them around for my chooks. If you want to spray grasshoppers, try Neem oil, Yates Natrasoap or a homemade or commercial chilli, garlic and soap mix.

MEALYBUG

Description: Mealybugs are really ugly bugs that suck the sap out of your plants, which weakens and can kill your plant. You know you have mealybugs when you see lots of cottonwool-like material specially around new growth. New growth will also become distorted

Mealybug
Rohanne Young

How to deal with them: My favourite way of dealing with mealybug is to encourage ladybeetles into my garden. Their larvae look just like the mealybug except that they can move on their own. If you see a mealybug "walking" then it's actually a Ladybeetle larvae. If you don't have them naturally in your garden, buy in some ladybeetle larvae. If you want to spray, I find the Yates Natrasoap, most effective against mealybug. For severe cases use a double strength solution of Natrasoap with one or two drops of vegetable oil. You could also try a homemade or commercial chilli, garlic and soap mix.

NEMATODES

Description: Generally known as root knot nematodes these are tiny parasitic worms that infect the roots of vulnerable plants. They cause the plants to develop a gall or knot that prevents them being able to take up any nutrients. The plants will then look wilted as if they need water but won't recover after watering and will collapse and die fairly quickly. Nematodes affect a wide variety of plants but are a huge problem with tomatoes in the home garden

Nematode from Rhonda's garden
Rhonda Binns

How to deal with them: Nematodes are a nasty pest, as once plants are infected a lot of other pests and diseases are attracted to the ailing plant. The recommended treatment for nematodes is crop rotation so that you starve the nematode worm. It is also good to fumigate the soil with a green manure of mustard as these plants contains isocyanates, which break down to isocyanide, fumigating the soil. I prefer the Red Asian mustard as it is hotter and contains more isocyanates. You also need to add plenty of good organic matter, as this introduces and supports many of the beneficial bacteria that will attack the nematode worm. You can make a drench to treat the soil. The drench is made using 8 litres of warm water, ½ cup of black strap molasses and 1 litre full cream milk. Mix together and apply generously to the soil each week for 8 weeks.

RED SPIDER MITE

Description: Red Spider Mite, also known as the two spotted mite, will suck the sap out of your plants, which will weaken your plant and can kill it. You know you have mites when the leaves of your plants look mottled and you notice fine spider webbing, especially on the under-side of leaves. The photo shows a bad case with the webbing clearly visible.

Red spider mite with webbing
Pixabay

How to deal with them: mites is to mist the plants regularly, especially in the late afternoon or evening as mites like hot, dry conditions. If you have a bad infestation you could try buying in some predatory mites which will eat the red spider mite. If you want to spray try Eco-oil, Neem oil, Yates Success or Natrasoap or with a homemade or commercial chilli, garlic and soap mix. A simple water and detergent mix applied a couple of times a day may also help.

SCALE

Description: Scale are bugs that suck the sap out of your plants, which weakens and can kill your plant. You know when you have Scale as you will notice hard brown, or grey bumps or soft white or green bumps along the stems and along the veins of leaves.

Brown Scale
Rohanne Young

How to deal with them: Scale is really destructive. They are an insect that is very difficult to deal with organically! To deal with scale you can try buying in some predatory ladybeetle larvae (especially the red chilorus) which will eat the scale. If you want to spray, try Neem oil, Eco pest oil, Yates Natrasoap or a homemade mix of chilli, garlic and soap. I am currently trying diatomaceous earth as a barrier around plants. I find that the ants can't cross this barrier as scale need the ants to move them as they don't have any legs.

SNAILS AND SLUGS

Description: Slugs and snails will eat your plants, often attacking the plant at soil level and killing young seedlings almost instantly. Since I have been living in the tropics and sub-tropics I have had much fewer problems with slugs and snails. When I was gardening in Canberra they were in plague proportions! You know when you have slugs and snails as you will see the slime they leave on the plant leaves, on pathways and on the soil.

Snails
Rohanne Young

How to deal with them: The best way I found to deal with slugs and snails was to go out after dark, especially after it had rained, and collect all the snails and slugs in a milk container that was half filled with a strong salt water solution. I found after a few nights the numbers plummeted. If you don't want to do this try spreading coffee grounds, sawdust, ground eggshells or cinnamon powder around your plants, as the slugs won't crawl across this barrier. Another solution involves leaving beer traps dug into the ground. The slugs are attracted to the beer smell, fall into the trap and drown. A lot of people swear by this trap, but I didn't have a lot of luck with it.

THRIPS

Description: Thrips are tiny sap sucking insects. They are normally about a centimetre in size, though they can get up to 1.5 cms. I have only had a thrip invasion once in my vegetable garden, and they totally decimated my snake beans! Like all sap sucking insects, they work by injecting a poison into the growing tip of your plant which leads to weakened and distorted growth

Thrip in garden
Rohanne Young

How to deal with them: Thrips are best controlled by good garden hygiene, i.e. removing all dying and dead matter from your garden, especially in autumn as they will overwinter in this debris. Spray with either Eco pest oil or Neem oil to control thrip during an attack.

60. My plant is looking sick. Does it have a disease and how do I treat it?

There are a number of common diseases that can affect plants in your vegetable garden. The disease that I have the most problem with is powdery mildew. I have given up even trying to grow cucumbers in summer, as they always get powdery mildew and become all withered and then they die.

Some insects like ladybeetles will eat the powdery mildew and these should be really encouraged. Some varieties of pumpkin and zucchini are more resistant to powdery mildew than others and, if you are having problems like I do, then you should seek out the more resistant varieties.

Capsicum with blossom end rot
Rohanne Young

Another common disease of vegetables is called Blossom end rot. Blossom end rot affects plants like tomatoes and capsicum and occurs mostly when plants have not been watered as regularly as they would like. It can also indicate a deficiency of calcium in the soil. I have had blossom end rot, mostly on capsicum and it can be really disheartening. To deal with this make sure that you have a regular watering schedule and apply some dolomite lime to the soil.

If you want to persevere with growing pumpkins, squash, zucchini and cucumber, and your plants do end up with powdery mildew, then the best spray is to mix a 50:50

solution of full cream milk and water in a spray bottle. Apply this to the leaves of the plant, making sure you spray both sides of the leaves to be really effective.

Another treatment you can try is sulphur powder, dusted on the leaves. Make sure you wear a mask while applying the powder so it doesn't irritate your eyes and mouth.

You can also make a natural fungicide, by mixing 1 tablespoon baking soda, 1 tablespoon Eco pest oil and 1 to 2 drops dishwashing liquid. Add this to a litre of water and spray both sides of the leaf. Commercial fungicides are also available but some of these are pretty nasty. Try and use an eco-fungicide which works on changing the pH of the leaves so the fungus is no longer able to grow.

The other common disease that I have battled with in my garden is rust. Rust is caused by fungi and these fungi need healthy plant material to thrive. You can tell when you have rust disease on your plants, as bright yellow/orange pimples will be present on the undersides of the leaves. In the vegetable garden rust can affect beans, spinach and silverbeet. I have had problems mostly with rust on silverbeet.

Rust is fairly difficult to treat and eradicate as the spores are spread by wind and by water splashes. Rust spores over-winter in the soil only to reappear when the weather warms up. It is best to prevent the spread of rust by collecting any affected leaves and solarising them in a plastic bag in the sun. When watering your vegetables make sure that you don't water overhead as the water droplets will carry the spores. Drip systems work best for vegetables.

61. You mean there are good bugs! What are these?

When I first started gardening I used to hear about bugs and instantly assume that this meant a pest attack on my plants. It was only in relatively recent times that I became aware that there were just as many good bugs, helping you fight the bad bugs, as there are bugs that will damage your plants.

It seems strange now but I grew up being almost scared of praying mantis. They look very weird and I was told that if they were human-size they could kill us, which is true! Luckily they aren't human-size and they do an amazing job in the garden, eating insects such as grasshoppers, caterpillars, moths and crickets.

Many of the bugs in our gardens are actually essential for plant growth. These bugs help pollinate flowers, create and spread seeds, as well as kill the harmful bugs that are eating our plants. Good bugs include helpful insects like bees, ladybeetles, hoverflies, praying mantis and micro wasps. Even wasps can fall into the good-guy category!

These bugs will be present in any healthy garden and will help you control the bad bugs that are eating your plants. However, they need something to feed on! So you need to have some of the pesky bugs, to ensure that the good bugs come into your garden.

The worst thing that you can do is to try and eliminate all pests that are eating your plants through the use of pesticides and insecticides, because these chemicals do not discriminate. They kill all the good bugs just as effectively as they kill the bad bugs.

It is far better for you, your garden and planet earth, to let good bugs do your dirty work. Below is a picture of some of these good bugs that I have found in my garden, along with a description of what they do and how they help in my garden.

ASSASSIN BUGS

Description: Assassin bugs are generally orange to rusty brown in colour. The adult bugs have translucent wings, but the nymphs don't have wings and can't fly. The bugs are so named as they hide in bark and foliage and sneak up on their prey, often attacking it from the rear. They inject their prey with and enzyme which liquifies the organs, killing the bug.

Assassin bug eggs
Ann Roffey

What good do they do: Assassin bugs have a huge appetite and are voracious eaters. They eat any insects they can catch, including aphids, caterpillars, grasshoppers and beetles. Unfortunately they are pretty indescriminate, so will also catch and kill some beneficial insects, particularly bees, which are their favourite food! However, given their voracious appetite and the fact that they kill a large number of bad bugs, they are generally considered to be good guys in your garden.

BEES

Description: I think everyone knows what a bee is! Bees are flying insects. There are thousands of different varieties of bees. Most people will recognise the black and yellow striped colours of the worker honey bees, although bees come in many other colours and sizes. There are native bees, which as the name suggests are native to the country of origin, including the blue banded bee at left which is native to Australia and a resident in my garden. There are also a number of varieties of honey bees, known variously as European bees, Italian bees or just plain honey bees.

Blue banded bee on sage
Rohanne Young

What good do they do: Bees are essential to the pollination of plants. Without bees much of our fruits and vegetables would not be produced. If you are trying to grow tomato, eggplants, capsicum, pumpkins or myriad of other edible plants, and they are producing flowers but not giving you fruit, then there is a good chance that you have a shortage of bees in your garden. This is easily fixed by buying in a native bee hive or contacting a hive keeper and seeing if they want to agist their hives in your garden. You can also try hand pollinating, where you take the male plant and dust the female stamen with the pollen. However I much prefer encouraging beneficial insects such as bees into my garden to do all the hard work for me!

HOVERFLY

Description: Hoverflies are flying insects about 0.5 to 1 cm in size. It took me quite a while to realise these weren't just immature honey bees as they look a little like a miniature worker bee, being mostly yellow and black striped. They hover around your plants looking for food including nectar, pollen and bugs. Now that I have found out what they are, and how useful they are, I love seeing them in my garden.

Hoverfly
Rohanne Young

What good do they do: The adult hoverfly feeds on the nectar of plants. It is only in recent years that we have started to realise how important they are in also pollinating plants. They play a key role in plant pollination and can actually make up for bee deficiencies in your garden to some extent. The hoverfly larvae have a voracious appetite and feed on sap-sucking insects including aphids, scale and thrips

LACEWING

Description: I used to see Lacewings in my garden all the time and, not knowing what they were, thought they were doing my plants damage. It couldn't be further from the truth! Lacewings are flying insects varying in size from less than 1cm up to 5 cm in length. They generally have a bright green body with 4 translucent lacy wings. Both the adult and their larvae have voracious appetites and eat aphids, mealybug and thrips.

Lacewing
Rohanne Young

What good do they do: The adult lacewing is really beautiful with almost translucent wings, hence the name. They are a seriously good guy in your garden as the adult will feed on nectar and pollen as well as soft bodied insects including aphids and mites. The larvae of lacewings have enormous appetites and feed on aphids, mites and caterpillars. You can buy lacewing larvae easily online.

LADY BEETLE

Description: I grew up with Ladybeetles. I think every child has a beautiful idea of ladybeetles. They just look the part with their bright red spotty body. Traditionally they are thought of as being about 0.5 to 1 cm in size, with a domed body and red coloured wings with 3 black spots on each wing, six short legs and a black head, although there are many other species with stripes or even without colour. Some types of ladybeetles feed on aphids and other bugs while another type of ladybeetle is great for cleaning up fungi like powdery mildew.

Ladybeetle
Rohanne Young

What good do they do: The adult ladybeetle feeds primarily on aphids and is estimated to consume over 5,000 aphids a year!! However, if you encourage them into your garden they will lay heaps of eggs and the larvae will eat through a huge amount of mealybug and aphids or powdery mildew! Just be aware of the 28 spotted ladybeetle as they are the vegetarians of the family and prefer to feast on your plants, damaging the leaves and stems.

LADY BEETLE LARVAE

Description: Ladybeetle larvae come in a range of colours and sizes from white through to orange and black with orange heads. They start tiny, about 0.5 mm in size, and can grow to about a centimetre before turning into an adult Ladybeetle.

Ladybeetle larvae
Rohanne Young

What good do they do: Ladybeetle larvae eat a huge amount of aphids, but they have a more varied diet and also eat mealybugs, mites, scale and other soft small pest insects. They are one of the best mealybug controls a gardener can welcome into their garden. In fact, when dealing with mealybug make sure you differentiate them from the ladybeetle larvae! They look so similar, if you are not careful you might kill one of the good guys! The main difference between mealybug and ladybeetle larvae is that the larvae can move by itself, so will "walk" toward its prey whereas the mealybug has no legs and relies on ants to move it.

MICRO WASPS

Description: Micro wasps are tiny flying insects that are great allies in your garden. The larvae of micro wasps bury themselves in the body of cabbage moth and other caterpillars and eat the caterpillar from the inside out. Quite gruesome, but fascinating to watch! Unlike normal wasps the micro wasps don't sting humans, which as an allergy suffer is a great bonus!

Microwasp eggs
Rohanne Young

What good do they do: Micro wasps play a huge role in your garden. You might not always see them but it is important you do what you can to encourage them. They are excellent predators of caterpillars and lay their eggs inside the caterpillar and consume the caterpillar from the inside. They don't kill the caterpillar until they are ready to hatch. I still haven't "knowingly" seen a micro-wasp, but I regularly come across their egg stacks!

NATIVE BEES

Description: It has only been in relatively recent times that I have become aware of our native bees. I grew up believing all bees were yellow and brown striped and produced honey. It was a shock to learn that there are over 1,500 species of native bees in Australia. Many of them are solitary bees, meaning that they don't live in colonies. The exception is the native stingless bees as they live in hives in temperate and subtropical areas. These bees are tiny, generally about a third the size of a normal house fly. They are called stingless bees because they don't sting. Being allergic to normal bee stings, I am a huge fan of our native stingless bees.

Stingless Native bees
Rohanne Young

What good do they do: Native bees play a huge role in plant pollination. Once in your garden they will pollinate everything! Even flowers that you don't want pollinated such as weeds! They are especially good at pollinating mangoes, macadamias and lychees in your sub-tropical garden. In your edible garden you will often see the small native bees flying around your flowering plants and helping with pollination. They are really tiny but they do a huge amount of work!

PRAYING MANTIS

Description: Like most children I grew up being fascinated and a little bit scared of praying mantis insects. The variety most commonly seen in the garden are green or brown and vary in size from around 6cm to more than 10cm. They have a triangular shaped head with a long torso and long back legs. The elongated front legs are held upright, which is where the common name comes from. Praying mantis have wings but generally only the male can fly.

Praying mantis
Rohanne Young

What good do they do: The adult praying mantis plays an important part in keeping pests under control in your garden. Adults live on flies, crickets, moths including the white cabbage moth, caterpillars, grasshoppers and other insects, making them a useful part of the balanced garden.

PRAYING MANTIS LARVAE

Description: The praying mantis will lay its eggs in a small sack on the underside of leaves (see photo at left). The sack looks like a miniature paper balloon. When it hatches you can get hundreds of minute praying mantis climbing down from the sack and onto your plants.

Praying mantis egg sac
Sharon Kennedy

What good do they do: The larvae of praying mantis when they hatch will number in the hundreds. They have a voracious appetite and will eat aphids, mites, mosquitoes and gnats making them a significant part of the balanced garden. Whenever I see them now, I collect praying mantis in the hope that they will lay an egg sack in my garden.

WASPS

Description: I think most people have heard of wasps and they have a pretty scary, and well-earned reputation! Wasps are flying insects that are closely related to bees. They are generally more aggressive than bees and, unlike bees, they can sting you multiple times. Wasps don't collect nectar or make honey, but they do pollinate plants when moving from plant to plant. They generally have smooth, shiny torsos without the hairs that bees have to collect nectar and pollen.

Wasp
Rohanne Young

What good do they do: Wasps have a pretty bad reputation as they will sting any intruder, to protect their hives. However, what many gardeners do not know, even people who have been gardening for a long time is that wasps play an important role in the garden. They are excellent predators of caterpillars and lay their eggs inside the caterpillar and consume the caterpillar from the inside. They also play a role in pollination for plants that need "buzz" stimulation to be pollinated.

By attracting these natural predators to your garden, you will ensure that your garden is in balance. The best way to attract good bugs is to plant some insect-attracting plants in among your vegetables and herbs.

Plants such as calendula, coriander, dill and cosmos are all good for attracting beneficial insects. Many of these plants are termed umbelliferous plants, as their flowers look a bit like an inverted umbrella, with many tiny flowers that attract these small insects. These plants also help the beneficial insects by providing them with a varied diet including nectar, as well as the water, which they also need to survive.

Chapter 11

VISITORS AND GATECRASHERS

This Chapter is about how to deal with beneficial visitors as well as gate crashers in your garden.

One of the gatecrashers in Carolyn's garden
Carolyn Hurley

62. What about other visitors to my garden? Can frogs, skinks, lizards and spiders help in my garden?

Apart from good and bad bugs, there is a raft of other animals that live in our gardens. These include reptiles, rodents, spiders and birds. I have both blue tongue lizards and other lizards and skinks, as well as frogs and toads and snakes. My garden has also recently welcomed a family of Kookaburras.

Living in the sub-tropics, there are lots and lots of garden skinks of varying sizes in my garden. They range in size from less than 2 cm up 14 cm in length. They are often golden or bronze in colour, although they can also be silver, spotted or striped. Skinks have a pretty big appetite and eat moths, slaters, flies and their maggots, caterpillars, grasshoppers, cockroaches, earwigs, slugs, small spiders, ants and many other small insects. I actively encourage them in my garden as they are seriously good guys.

The best way to attract and keep these visitors in your garden is to ensure that there are places for them to hide from predators, to sun themselves, water to drink and plenty of insects that they can feed on. It is important to have some leaf litter in your garden as it is often used as a quick hide-out for skinks and lizards trying to evade capture by birds and other predators.

Another visitor to my garden that I love is my green tree frogs and my stripey marsh frogs. Frogs eat the larvae of insects including mosquito larvae, helping you control the insect population. They are also an excellent indicator of the health of your garden, as frogs cannot survive in gardens where lots of pesticides, herbicides and other poisons are used.

However, I am not keen on cane toads. To me they are an introduced pest that out-competes our native frogs and toads for food. I used to just leave them be, but they breed rapidly, so I go through periods where I go out in the garden at night and spray them with Dettol. In the morning I collect all the dead toads. They are pretty easy to find as the Dettol smell is a dead give-away!

I used to be seriously scared of spiders. As far as I was concerned the only good spider was a dead spider! I actually underwent hypnotherapy to try and help me cope with spiders. I have since learnt that all I really needed to do was to discover just how seriously good spiders are and how necessary they are in a healthy garden.

I now encourage golden orb spiders to weave their web in my garden. The golden orb that lives above my cycad fern catches all the blue cycad moths, so I never have chewed fronds. It is funny though how many tradesmen come to my place and are seriously scared of spiders!

I know that I have at least one snake living in my garden, probably more! Snakes are curious creatures in that they actually don't often let you know that they are around. The snake I know about in my garden is a green tree snake. He happily lives down near my second compost bin and every so often I will go to put some compost in the bin and disturb him. He is well over a metre long and quite plump so he is obviously thriving.

To help make your garden a welcoming home for skinks, lizards, frogs and other animals it is best to minimise the use of most garden chemicals such as pesticides and weed killers. Even some chemicals that you might not expect to have an adverse effect on skinks, lizards and frogs can be harmful. These include many lawn weed and feed products, some inorganic fertilisers, weed killers based on Glyphosate, household fly spray, termite sprays well as the obvious pesticides and insecticides.

By poisoning insects, you risk poisoning all the good visitors to your garden, but more importantly, you remove their food source. If you can tolerate a low level of bad bugs in your garden, you will encourage nature to come up with a solution that is cheaper, and more effective, than most pesticides which need regular re-application.

63. What can I do about destructive visitors to my garden like possums, cats and rodents?

I recently suffered through a rat plague in my garden and let me assure you, they are not fun! In my experience they are the most destructive gatecrashers that you can have in your garden. They eat everything! And when they have run out of all your vegetables and herbs they will dig up the roots, eat your potatoes, yakon and jicama, even eat young trees. They have killed 2 of my pawpaw trees! I would much prefer a possum. Compared to rats, possums are well behaved!

I have tried just about every possible way to get rid of rats. I have tried feeding them toothpaste and dried potato, both of which are supposed to kill them without harming the environment. I was not successful with either method. The best solution is probably rat traps. Try the newer versions, which are made of plastic and have savage teeth! The other solution is the cage where rats enter and can't exit. If you have a reptile collector then offer the rats to them. Otherwise you have to drown them. In my area it is actually illegal to relocate live rats off your property!

Other destructive visitors to your garden can include possums, kangaroos, rabbits and even deer in some parts of Australia. Luckily in Queensland we don't have rabbits, but I have a resident possum. I also get the occasional visit from fruit bats and flying foxes when the mango tree has fruit.

There are some chemical deterrents, often based on pheromones that are supposed to help deter these animals. These work on the animal's sense of smell and these can be sprayed on, or scattered around the plants that you don't want eaten. The problem with many of these deterrents is that they have to be reapplied each time it rains, so I haven't found them to be very effective.

There is a new possum deterrent that works on changing the taste of the leaves. It makes them bitter to the possums and they leave those plants alone. I have been trialing this deterrent in my vegetable patch and so far I have been very impressed with the results. However, I also leave out small pieces of fruit for the possum, as I do realize that he needs to eat and was probably here before I moved in!

With the flying foxes and bats that come to feed on your fruit trees, I have found the best solution to be a solar floodlight. The bats and flying foxes don't like the light so they will change their flight path and stop feeding on your fruit. You do need to make sure that all of the tree is covered, otherwise they will quickly locate any fruit that is in the dark!

Some wild birds may also have the occasional snack on your fruit trees, but I have found that these are often more interested in the bugs feeding on your trees and are therefore helping you! I did have a sulphur-crested cockatoo who took up temporary residence in my garden when the passionfruit vine was laden with fruit. He only ate one fruit a day, and he ate it so thoroughly that I only realized he was there by finding small pieces of the passionfruit skin on the ground. Then I actually saw him in action. We came to tolerate each other, and he moved on when the vine finished fruiting.

Even though they can be destructive, some of these visitors can also be of benefit to your garden, so it is important to figure out what level of exclusion you want to aim for. Flying foxes and bats are important in the pollination of dragon fruit and other fruits, while birds are great at eating a lot of the insects that attack your garden.

If you decide that you need to totally keep these visitors out of your garden (I don't, but then I have not had my whole garden eaten by rabbits or deer), the most effective way is to construct sturdy fences. Small areas can also be protected using a low-voltage electric fence, powered by a car battery. These can be purchased online or created by the home-handyman.

In bad cases you may need to cover vegetable patches and fruit trees with anti-bird netting. You can construct an effective net and frame over your herb and vegetable patch using spare irrigation poly-pipe domed-over and buried each side into the soil. Netting can then be draped over and secured using tent pegs or rocks. You will need a sturdy metal or wooden rod inside the pipe at ground level otherwise the poly-pipe can soften in hot weather, collapsing the netting onto your plants. However, I find that netting can also keep out many of the beneficial insects, thereby impacting on your overall crop, so proceed with caution.

When using netting to keep out possums and flying foxes, make sure that you use approved netting with small holes so that the animals claws and wings don't get trapped. Also, make sure the netting is stretched tightly to stop animals getting caught in loose nets.

Chapter 12

WAYS TO GROW FOOD WITHOUT CHEMICALS

This Chapter is about how to get healthy with your edible garden, and covers some of the ways you can grow foods naturally without chemical interference.

Growing plants in water
Rohanne Young

64. What is companion planting and how do I do it?

One of the fundamental ideas of companion planting is to work with nature, and to plant as nature would do. In essence, companion planting is the practice of growing plants together for the positive advantage of both plants.

I use companion planting regularly in my garden. Ever since I realised that the concept of growing vegetables in rows was so against what would happen naturally, not to mention that it provided a veritable landing strip for the bugs!

Now I have vegetables and herbs growing all throughout the garden, with flowers growing in my vegetable patch alongside the vegetables, which is one of the principles of companion planting.

It concerns me when people say "I don't want to do companion planting because I don't want to grow flowers", or "I tried companion planting and it didn't work". Companion planting is not an exact science. Nor is it a cure-all for everything that can go wrong in your garden.

Companion planting is also a lot more involved than just planting a few marigolds to fend off nematodes in the roots of your tomatoes. I believe that companion planting can be grouped into nine main categories or benefits.

These are:

1. Attract beneficial insects to your vegetable garden by providing food and nectar. Flowers such as marigolds, sunflowers, sweet alyssum and calendula perform this function well, as do several herbs such as coriander, parsley and dill if they are allowed to flower and go to seed;
2. Keep away the bad bugs and diseases, either by emitting a strong smell that swamps the smell of tempting fresh vegetables or by fumigating the soil to disrupt pests like nematodes. Marigolds perform both these functions well, as do the herbs mint and rue. Mustard is great for fumigating the soil and killing off nematodes;
3. Visually confuse pests by disguising the shape of desirable vegetables. Many bugs actually search for their preferred crops based on what they look like! For example, if you plant leeks alongside your cabbages, the white cabbage moth may not identify the cabbage shape because of the taller leeks growing alongside and among the cabbages;
4. Act as a sacrificial plant that gets eaten instead of your prized plants. Land cress is a great sacrificial plant as the white cabbage moth prefers to lay its eggs on this plant, which is toxic to the young caterpillars;
5. Increase plant growth by improving access to nutrients. Peas, beans and other legumes assist with this by fixing nitrogen from the air and making it available to plants who can't do this. Planting deep rooted vegetables like carrots and herbs such as comfrey, also helps as these plants bring nutrients up closer to the surface of the soil, allowing more shallow rooted plants to access the nutrients;
6. Reduce water usage, as well as control weeds, by providing a green mulch that smothers out weeds. Good mixed plantings will achieve this, with lettuce happily growing under basil and tomatoes to keep weeds away from all plants;

7. Enhance the flavours of each crop. Basil and tomatoes work well together in this combination;
8. Stunt the growth of other plants. Garlic and onion are good at emitting chemicals that can stunt other plants' growth. Corn and tomatoes are another of these combinations, where both plants will be stunted if grown together in close proximity;
9. Provide shade and staking, such as planting beans, cucumbers and corn together. This is a classic companion planting combination. The beans climb up the corn, and help provide the corn with nitrogen, while the corn provides shade to the cucumber, which in turn keeps the shallow roots of the corn cool.

The best way to take advantage of companion planting is to vary your planting so that you don't have too many of each vegetable in one place. This way, if the bad bugs find one or two of your plants they may miss the rest of the crop, saving you from losing your whole season's planting.

It is also best to plant vegetables and herbs with different nutrient requirements together, so they are not competing for nutrients. Similarly, grow shallow rooted plants with deeper rooted plants so they complement, rather than compete, for nutrients.

A few companion planting combinations that I regularly use, and have found to be effective, include:

1. Mustard grown with tomatoes - I have never had a problem with nematodes;
2. Lettuce with everything - it is very shallow rooted so keeps other plants cool as well as being an effective weed control;
3. Marigolds with cabbage, bok choy and other green, leafy vegetables - helps control the caterpillars of the white cabbage moth butterfly;
4. Calendula with cabbage, bok choy and other green, leafy vegetables - helps control the caterpillars of the white cabbage moth butterfly;
5. Basil and parsley with asparagus - leads to more asparagus spears and a better crop;
6. Beetroot and silverbeet - when grown together seem to confuse the white cabbage moths and caterpillars;
7. Leeks with cabbage and cauliflower - confuses the white cabbage moth butterflies and caterpillars.

65. What about crop rotation? Do I really need to rotate my vegetables to different garden beds each year?

Crop rotation, by its very name, tells you that this method has come to us from the commercial farming sector. It is based on the practice of intensive commercial farming where it was found that planting the same crop in the same place year after year made it easier for insects and soil-borne diseases to attack the plants, reducing the amount harvested.

This practice has become reasonably well established in the home garden as well, with the assumption that it will help with the amount of food you can produce.

However, this practice does not really allow for those of us who are growing our vegetables on a single allotment, in a very small garden, or even just in pots or on balconies.

I have to be honest here and admit that I don't act in accordance with the practices of crop rotation. I prefer to use a mixture of biological gardening practices and companion planting practices across all my garden beds rather than having separate areas set aside for distinct crops. Biological gardening does not separate food plants out into groups which are then grown in rows, but takes a more natural approach. In biological gardening, the herbs and vegetables are planted randomly, along with flowers and other non-food bearing plants.

Although I understand some of the principles such as planting nutrient enriching crops such legumes after nutrient hungry crops such as corn, by interplanting these crops this work can be done on every planting.

This makes it more difficult for insects to destroy your plants, and also acts on the fact that some plants naturally strengthen and support each other, while others are natural enemies, which is the basis of companion planting.

However, if you choose to use crop rotation, it pays to set up a structured system. The most common system that I have seen works on a 5 bed rotation:

    Bed 1 is for green manure;
    Bed 2 is for leaf crops;
    Bed 3 is for flowering crops;
    Bed 4 is for fruiting crops; and
    Bed 5 is for root crops.

To work well, you will need to keep accurate records of what you planted, when it was planted, how well it grew and any pests or diseases, so that you can plan what you want to plant next and where you are going to plant it. There are some excellent Apps available to help with keeping these records and planning your garden.

66. I've heard people talk about gardening by the moon cycles. What is this about?

Gardening by the cycles of the moon, or moon gardening, is a very old tradition that has been used in various cultures for centuries. To understand moon gardening you have to first understand that the moon has four main phases.

The first and second phases occur when the moon is "waxing" or growing from a sliver of a new moon up to the full moon. The third and fourth phases happen when the moon is "waning" or moving away from the full moon back down to the last sliver.

Each phase, known as quarters, lasts for around 7 days. With moon gardening these phases are used to determine when above ground crops or below ground crops are planted and harvested.

In the waxing phases the sap rises in plants, which makes these times best for planting crops that are harvested for the parts of the plant that grow above the ground. This includes green leafy vegetables, herbs, tomatoes and other vegetables that produce fruit such as capsicum, corn, peas and beans.

The waxing moon phases are also the best time to prune your fruit trees and other perennial plants after they have finished flowering and fruiting.

Once the full moon is reached, and through to the third quarter is the best time for sowing or planting out crops that are harvested for their roots such as carrots, parsnips, beetroot, potatoes as well as asparagus which requires healthy roots to produce spears. It is also a good time for taking cuttings and dividing your plants. Note: these should also be in accordance with the proper seasons for planting each crop.

Under the principles of moon gardening you should avoid planting during the final quarter of the moon and, instead, use this time to tidy the garden and perform tasks that will help improve your soil. You should also avoid planting for 12 hours before and after the moon changes from one phase to the next.

If you want to try moon gardening you will need to obtain an accurate moon chart that is relevant to where you live and your climate zone. I find the moon cycles on their own are too restrictive, and prefer to use the systems advocated under biodynamic gardening (refer Question 68).

Even if you don't agree that the phases of the moon affect the flow of sap within plants, you can try using the moon cycles as a way of managing the jobs in your garden. At least this way you get a justifiable break from all the work you need to do in the garden, and you don't feel like you have to get everything finished right now!

67. What is permaculture and how do I use it in my garden?

Permaculture is a system of gardening using many of the same practices that underpin organic and biological gardening, as I mentioned at the start of this book.

Permaculture varies from biological and organic gardening in that it doesn't just look at your garden as an environment in isolation, but it also includes your house, the clothes you wear, the materials you use, energy production and your energy usage, whether you harvest rainwater and your water use.

Permaculture extends the focus of your garden to also consider your community and the broader environmental impacts that we all have, as well as the impacts that the environment, including weather and climate, can have on your house and garden.

I have found it difficult to apply some of the principles of permaculture, as I live in a house that was built without these principles in mind. However, that doesn't mean I can't adopt other permaculture practices.

A simple way to introduce some of the principles of permaculture into your life starts with growing some of your own food. Even in a small way this can make a difference, as it is estimated that more than one third of our ecological footprint is taken up by the food we buy.

Permaculture can be hard to describe in simple terms as there are no quick fixes, and each solution depends largely on the particular piece of land or farm or community where you choose to live. When you start down the permaculture pathway it can quickly become a complete lifestyle, not just a way of gardening!

While some of its principles can be used very successfully in the home garden, to be truly committed involves the adoption of the whole design philosophy, which has 12 underlying principles:

1. Observe and interact – engage with nature to design solutions that suit your particular situation.
2. Catch and store energy – collect resources when they are abundant so you can use them in times of need.
3. Obtain a yield – achieve useful rewards as part of the working you are doing.
4. Apply self regulation and accept feedback – any good system requires a feedback loop which discourages unsuitable actions and modifies practices when they don't perform as expected.
5. Use and value renewable resources and services – alter our behaviours and reduce our dependence on non-renewable resources.
6. Produce no waste – ensure nothing goes to waste by valuing and making use of all the resources that are available to us. This includes composting, re-using and recycling.
7. Design from patterns to details – use the patterns we observe in nature and society to form the backbone of our designs, with the details filled in as we go.
8. Integrate rather than segregate – use the relationships that naturally develop between systems and resources to ensure they work together to support each other.
9. Use small and slow solutions – make better use of local resources and produce more sustainable outcomes.
10. Use and value diversity – reduce vulnerability to threats and take advantage of the unique nature of the environment in which it resides by valuing diversity.
11. Use edges and value the marginal – the most valuable, diverse and productive elements in the system occur at the interface between things. Observe and use these margins.
12. Creatively use and respond to change – inevitable change can be positively impacted by carefully observing and then intervening at the right time.

Although we can't all build our own houses from their foundations or grow all our own food, we can make choices about what we eat, how it is produced and transported.

In this way we can help to conserve the environment and reduce our own environmental impacts.

68. What is biodynamic gardening and how can I use this in my garden?

When I first heard about Biodynamic (BD) gardening I must admit that I thought it was a bit "out there". You know what I mean....pretty alternative. Not that there is anything wrong with alternative living, but for a gardener from the suburbs it took a little bit to understand and accept the concepts behind biodynamics.

Like organic gardening, it is based on the principles of growing food without the use of pesticides, herbicides or genetically modified organisms. However, biodynamics varies from straight organic gardening by working to optimise all forces of nature including the forces of the sun, moon, the planets and subterranean forces.

Basically, you take the ideology of moon gardening, and then you add in the 12 planets of the zodiac and use this to plan all your planting and gardening practices. Weird for some I am sure.

Like moon gardening, biodynamic gardening has set times for planting and harvesting food, based on the phases of the moon. However, by incorporating the forces of the other 12 planets, the actual days and times for planting and harvesting are much more lenient, with cycles generally taking 7 days instead of up to 28 days as happens with moon gardening.

At its foundation is a number of preparations including BD 500, which is made from cow manure that has been packed inside a cow horn, buried for 6 months before being dug up and used in extremely small concentrations. Microbes and worms convert the manure into a material that has the consistency of worm castings. This preparation is applied in microscopic droplets to your garden.

When I first told my sister that I had this biodynamic preparation that had to be stirred into water vigorously for an hour, changing directions regularly to ensure that it is thoroughly mixed and energised, and then applied during the full moon, which that night happened at 11.45 pm, I think my sister thought that I had really lost the plot. I am still not sure how it happens or why, but I can tell you that my soil has benefitted more than I would have imagined since I have started using this mixture.......and I too am a natural borne cynic!

There is also a fruit tree paste, which is made from cow manure mixed with organic bentonite clay and BD preparations. This needs to be painted onto the trunks of fruit trees annually. I find that if I paint the trunks before the fruit tree flowers, I get a much better flowering.

When I have told gardening friends about this mix, they say things like "Oh that's working because fruit trees need calcium which the clay is supplying".

However, that didn't explain to me why my tropical peach went from having 4 flowers before application and over 100 flowers within a fortnight of application! And this resulted in a follow-up bumper crop of fruit.

Other BD preparations include BD 501, which is energised silica as well as preparations made from yarrow, camomile, stinging nettle and dandelion. Biodynamic methods also make use of various weed teas to provide essential nutrients back into the soil, as well as preparations called "peppers" which help address imbalances that lead to weed and pest invasions.

If you want to incorporate biodynamic gardening practices into your garden, as a minimum you will need to obtain an accurate biodynamic planting chart. You may then decide to purchase the various preparations such as BD500 to apply to your garden.

If you are really game and you can find a reputable workshop then I encourage you to have a go at making and using some of your own biodynamic preparations. I am confident you won't be disappointed!

69. What is hydroponics and how do I use it in my garden?

Hydroponics is another method that aims to grow plants without the use of pesticides and herbicides. In hydroponics you grow the plants in a liquid solution, usually water, which has been enriched with all the minerals and macro-nutrients that a plant would normally obtain from the soil. I haven't personally utilised hydroponics to grow vegetables, although it is on my to-do list and I have researched it extensively.

The system I hope to install involves the use of polypipe that is wall mounted, combining hydroponics with vertical gardening. This involves cutting holes at regular intervals along the polypipe so that plants such as lettuce can be suspended in the enriched water.

As the plants are not growing in soil it is extremely important that the growing solution contains all the minerals and macro-nutrients that the plant needs, in the correct quantity and chemical composition. Nutrient solutions for use in hydroponic systems can be purchased from a hydroponics nursery (check for online suppliers) or, if you have experience or want to experiment you can make your own nutrient mix.

In most hydroponic systems, except for the smallest systems, you will need a pump to ensure that the nutrients are evenly distributed and are readily available to the plant. You will also need some way of adding oxygen to the water as most plant roots will drown without an adequate supply of oxygen.

If you want to try hydroponics, there are two main methods. In the first method the plants are grown in a holding framework so that their roots are suspended in the enriched water, while in the second method the plant's root system is supported by a growing medium like perlite, coco, clay pebbles or rockwool.

Gardeners who use hydroponic systems claim that they get a better harvest from their edible plants using these systems, with much fewer problems with pests and diseases. This is one of the reasons that I would really like to try this technique.

A supplement to hydroponics involves the addition of freshwater fish, and is known as Aquaponics. Several fish including barramundi, bass and perch are suitable, depending on water temperature and other conditions. The waste products from the fish feed the plants and the plants filter the water and clean it for the fish.

70. Can I grow plants in water alone?

Some of the first plants that I grew involved placing a cutting of the plant in a glass of water and watching the cutting grow roots. I started with really easy non-edible plants such as coleus, and then graduated to growing edible plants including herbs. This is really just a simple, small-scale form of hydroponics.

Herb cuttings can be grown in glass bottles, glass jars or even plastic bottles. Amber or dark coloured bottles or jars are best, as plant roots generally like to grow away from light. If you don't have any dark bottles you can wrap paper around the bottles and jars to keep the root zone in the dark. This will also help keep the water clean and clear from any algae.

Bottles with a narrower neck can be useful as they support the cuttings and keep them upright. However, you can also use wide-necked jars and cover the top with a piece of nylon stocking or fine wire netting such as flyscreen wire, with holes punched through to support the cuttings.

Herb cuttings can develop roots quickly in water, making them a popular and useful option for the kitchen window sill. You can use cuttings from your own garden or from friends or neighbours' gardens. You can also use the herbs you get from stores or markets. Make sure you remove the lower leaves of any cuttings, as these can rot and turn the water sour and your herbs will start to smell bad and die.

As with any other plants, you will need to add fertiliser occasionally. Liquid fertilisers developed for herbs and vegetables are best. However these need to be extremely diluted, way beyond the recommended dilutions on the label, as these recommendations allow for some of the nutrients being held by the soil. Water borne plants will need about a tenth of the concentration recommended for soil-borne plants.

71. What are wicking beds and can I use them in my garden?

Wicking beds are gardens that are created with an inbuilt water reservoir, and use the capillary action of the soil to move the water up to the root zone of the plants. They are basically like a large self-watering pot. The first wicking beds that I used were a simple production created using a polystyrene box, with the lid making up the water-soil barrier and some polypipe for the water inlet.

Wicking beds, when they are properly set up, use significantly less water than traditional vegetable gardens, and produce much better harvests. Weeds also become much less of a problem as the soil surface is never watered, so the weed seeds have problems getting established. Wicking beds also require much less frequent watering, due to the water reservoir.

Wicking beds can be a great alternative to raised garden beds for your vegetables, especially when your garden suffers from root competition from trees. They are also a great solution if you are stuck with a concrete or paved yard.

Wicking beds can be as small or large as you want. To set up a wicking bed you need the following:

1. waterproof container or container with a waterproof lining,
2. wood chip, scoria or clay pebbles to fill the water reservoir,
3. an overflow pipe and inlet pipe for the water,
4. weed mat or shade cloth to keep the soil from muddying the water,
5. soil with a lot of compost and organic material, and
6. your seedlings.

Normal potting mix does not contain enough organic matter for the wicking action to happen successfully, so if you are constrained to using potting mix then you will need to add quite a lot of coir peat or home-made compost.

Larger wicking beds can be created from large wooden crates or can be built the same as a raised garden bed, with a pond liner or similar material being used to create the water reservoir. When selecting the lining material for your wicking bed, do not be tempted to use black plastic, even though it is cheaper as it disintegrates quickly with age. It is also easy to split black plastic when digging, which will rupture your water reservoir and stop the system from working. You will then have to remove everything and start all over again.

Chapter 13

TIPS TO ENSURE YOUR PLANTS THRIVE

This Chapter is about how to lessen disappointments in your garden, ensuring that your plants survive and thrive

Mixed planting of herbs, vegetables and flowers

72. My plant just died! Why?

It really disheartens me when one of my plants die. And sometimes plants die, even when you have done everything right. If your plant has been growing really successfully for a while, maybe it has just reached the end of its natural life.

Earlier in the book I discussed the difference between annual and perennial plants. Many herbs including basil, coriander and parsley are annuals and are only meant to live for a single season. You will know if your plant has come to the end of its natural life, as many plants flower and set seed when coming to the end of their life cycle.

Make the most of them while they are here and, if you are growing heritage seeds, harvest the seeds so you can grow them again next year. This way the new plants you grow will have learnt all about the growing conditions at your place and they will grow even stronger.

However, if your plant died prematurely and it wasn't at the end of its life cycle, you should do a bit of investigating to find out why. If you don't explore this, you may spend quite a bit of money and energy replacing plants only to have future plants die in a similar way!

The main things to look for are factors like:

- acidity or alkalinity of your soil (i.e. soil pH),
- if your plant received enough water and food,
- were they in the right location for their sun or shade requirements,
- were any plants in competition for food or water, especially roots of large trees,
- were they affected by weedkillers/chemicals designed to poison plants,
- if other plants in the vicinity were likely to suppress growth, and
- if there were any pests or diseases that impacted your plant.

Pests and diseases do tend to attack plants that are already weakened by some of the above-mentioned factors, so I would look at these first as they may give you a clue to other factors. When considering pests and diseases, don't forget to consider some less obvious pests including rodents and possums.

Despite what people may think about their abilities or otherwise to grow plants, the cause of a plant's premature death will generally be one of the factors outlined above and not a case of your inability to grow a garden.

73. How do I keep my garden healthy?

If you have followed the information covered in this book, then your edible garden should be well on its way to being a healthy garden. So how do you keep it healthy? I have covered the basics, so if you continue to follow these practices you should be set.

Make sure you visit your vegetable and herb garden daily, pull out any weeds before they get hold, water daily in summer and less frequently in winter, use an organic liquid fertilizer fortnightly in summer and monthly in winter, deal with any pests or diseases as soon as you notice them and your edible garden should be well on the way to not just staying healthy but thriving.

And remember to stop and smell the.......... well, whatever it is you've decided to grow.

It is not fun if you just look at your garden and think of it in terms of how much work needs to be done! I know as I have fallen into this trap at times and this is one of the quickest deterrents I have found to growing your own foods. You need to look at your garden as a way of connecting with the earth and providing nourishment for you and your family.

74. Do I really have to clean the tools between jobs? Why?

If I had my time over again I think this would be one of the lessons I wished I had learnt earlier. Good gardening tools make our gardening tasks much easier, so it pays to buy the best you can afford and look after them to protect your investment.

This doesn't have to be onerous or massively time consuming. For example, tools should be cleaned after each use, as this helps keep pests and diseases, insect eggs and weed seeds from being accidentally spread around the garden. After use I tend to dip my secateurs in warm, soapy water or a diluted bleach solution and dry them. The blades can then be wiped with vegetable oil to prevent them from rusting.

It also pays to sharpen the blades regularly, as this will ensure the secateurs cut your plants cleanly and don't crush the stems, which can allow diseases to enter the plant. Sharpening can be as easy as using a knife sharpener or a sharpening stone, although I get this job done by a professional. There is a guy who comes to our local organic gardening meetings who sharpens tools. There is also a guy down at my local farmers market, so look around and you should be able to find someone.

Spades, forks, trowels and any other tools that come into contact with soil should be hosed off with water after each use. This will wash most garden soil and compost away easily. To prevent tools from rusting, I keep an oil and sand mix in a bucket and dip tools into this mix. You can create one yourself by mixing course sand and vegetable oil in a bucket and stirring. Sliding the tools in and out of that mixture will wipe off any muck, as well as coat the blade with a fine layer of oil to prevent rust.

If the wooden handles of your tools become rough and damaged they can be cleaned, then smoothed off with sandpaper, before polishing with a natural, protective oil or painting with a bright coloured outdoor paint. I prefer to paint mine as I find the bright colours easy to see when I've misplaced a tool in the garden.

75. What tool is that and how do I use it?

As I started to get into gardening in a more serious way I found I needed a few more dedicated tools than the old kitchen fork and scissors that I had been using to make do. I still use the old kitchen fork as I find it the perfect tool when planting seedlings.

There is a large assortment of garden tools you may decide to buy. I have found that if you buy good quality tools they tend to last longer than cheap tools.

Some of the tools I have found useful include:

i. **Hand trowels, cultivators and forks** - used to dig the soil when smaller scale digging is required. They are also useful for planting seedlings and digging out weeds.
ii. **Large garden forks** - used for digging, turning and breaking up clumps of soil, aerating grass and digging over your compost heap.
iii. **Spades** - used for digging, cutting edges and dividing plants. It is important to keep the blade sharp so the spade does the hard work, not you. Spades can be sharpened using a sharpening stone.
iv. **Shovels** - used for moving garden material such as compost, sand and dirt.
v. **Hoes** - used for weeding by cutting off the weed at soil level. Hoes are also used for carving out rows when planting vegetables and for spreading mulch in garden beds.
vi. **Compost aerator** - used to dig down into the compost heap to help turn the material and introduce air into the heap. They can significantly speed up the composting process. One of the best tools I've bought. I also use this for aerating my worm tubes.
vii. **Wheelbarrow** - used for transporting materials like compost, soil, plants and leaves etc around your garden.
viii. **Mattock or pickaxe** - used for heavy digging when creating holes for planting trees and shrubs. Also useful when digging out large roots.
ix. **Pitch Fork** - used for moving garden materials, particularly mulch and bark. Once you master a pitchfork you won't ever move mulch with a spade again!
x. **Rake** - used for clearing away leaves and garden waste, breaking up clumps of soil, and spreading mulch and compost.
xi. **Planting augur earth drill** - used to dig hollows in the soil where seedlings and shrubs are going to be planted. They are useful if your soil is hard and compacted.
xii. **Cordless drill** - used with planting augur to drill holes into compacted or root-bound soil.
xiii. **Pruning saw** - used to cut through branches with minimum effort. They are useful for pruning fruit trees.
xiv. **Pruning Shears and loppers** - used to cut tree branches and create hedges.
xv. **Secateurs** - essential for all your smaller cutting jobs in the garden. They can be used to prune flowers, herbs and small branches of fruit trees.

Other apparatus that can be useful in the garden include:

- plastic buckets for collecting weeds, making weed teas and transporting small amounts of compost or mulch;
- wooden stakes and trellises;
- wire and fabric strips for tying up climbing plants or supporting new trees until they become established;
- pots and seedling trays;

- shade-cloth for creating temporary shade structures;
- old umbrellas for temporary shade;
- netting including mesh bags for covering fruit to exclude fruit fly; and
- watering equipment including watering cans and hoses.

76. I have a plant in the wrong place. Can I relocate it without killing it?

The main reason I find for needing to relocate a plant is if the plant isn't thriving. This may be because it requires more sun, and surrounding plants have grown, creating shade. You might find that you just want to rearrange the garden, or you are renting and you need to move and take your garden with you.

I find the majority of plants can be moved as long as you are careful. If you are able to, it is better to wait until the plant is in hibernation or at least not growing actively, but sometimes this is not possible, for example when you are moving house at the end of a lease.

When transplanting a plant that is not in hibernation, I recommend that you water it well the night before with a seaweed solution diluted to the colour of strong tea. This will help protect your plant from stress.

When you dig up the plant, whether it is hibernation or not, try and keep as much of the root ball intact and try to keep as much soil as possible around the roots. This can mean digging up to a metre outside the plant's trunk to get as much root as possible for small trees and large shrubs.

Have the new location ready, with the hole prepared and the soil loosened. Place some home-made compost in the hole and place the plant immediately in its new location. By minimising the amount of time between uprooting and replanting you will maximise the chance of your plant surviving.

If the new location is not available, transplant your plant into a pot that is large enough to easily accommodate the root ball. If this is not possible, for example a large citrus, then you may be able to wrap the root ball in several layers of damp newspaper followed by either a hessian sack of a large plastic garden bag. Note that this is only a very temporary solution, although a friend managed to keep a lemon tree alive like this for over a month and it still relocated to its new home and thrived.

77. How do I repot a plant?

I grow a lot of plants in pots. This is partly so that I can move pots around to meet their sun and water requirements, but also because it allows me to create micro-climates that meet a particular plant's needs.

However, this does mean that some of these plants will outgrow the pot that they are in and need repotting. You may also need to repot a plant if the potting mix has broken down or, as happened to me once, the plant has become so root-bound that it actually broke the pot.

If you use plastic pots you may find that they just deteriorate over time as the sun makes the plastic brittle. In the subtropics this can happen in as little as a year, so I no lonnger use plastic pots!

To repot a plant that has become pot-bound you usually need a pot that is one to two sizes larger than the current pot. Then it is simply a matter of placing the pot where you want it to rest, placing some potting mix in the base, up to approximately one-third of the pot, removing the plant from its existing pot and placing it in the new upsized pot. Fill in around the sides and the top of the root ball with potting mix and compost and water immediately with a seaweed solution to reduce transplant shock and encourage root growth.

It is recommended that you place the pot at the preferred site before filling it with potting mix and the plant as, with the exception of small pots, the pot plant can be very heavy when potted up. This can make moving it very difficult. Don't be tempted to go up too many pot sizes either, as plants can go into shock and really struggle until the roots grow enough to compensate for the larger pot.

When repotting a plant, it is important that the surface of the root ball stays at approximately the same level as it was in the previous pot. Some plants can suffer from a fungal disease known as collar rot if you cover too much of the stem where the plant emerges from the soil.

If your plant is grafted, as most citrus trees are, then it is important to ensure that the graft remains above the surface of the soil. If the graft is buried it can result in the tree above the graft dying and the plant returning to the rootstock which will either not produce fruit or produce inedible or inferior fruit.

Many fruit trees including citrus trees like lime, lemon and grapefruit, as well as herbs such as Kaffir limes and Bay leaf trees can be successfully grown in large pots. This is great if you are renting and want to be able to take the plant(s) with you when you move.

So what do I do going forward?

Now that we have come to the end of the book, I hope that I have answered all your question and maybe even answered some questions that you didn't know to ask.

And I hope that you have successfully grown some of your own edible plants and you want to keep going.

So, how do you manage this going forward? Firstly, by remembering that most edible plants are annuals, so you are going to need to replace plants that have come to the end of their life cycle. I find I need to replant my vegetable garden about 4 times a year.

You may do this by ripping everything out, applying new compost, new fertiliser and then plant another crop that is compatible with the current season, or you may choose to plant a few seedlings every couple of weeks so that you are never without freshly grown vegetables.

Don't forget that you are going to need to get into the practice of visiting your vegetable garden regularly so that you can remove weeds, water the plants and keep on top of pests and diseases. Hopefully you will agree with me that the return on investment is well and truly worth it! A shop bought lettuce will never be good enough once you have tasted the way it's meant to taste, straight from your own garden!

To end....., my favourite quote is that your garden will return 50 times the investment you put into it. Not just with food but also the joy, peace and a spiritual retreat from a noisy world and hurried people.

The biggest obstacle to growing a garden is taking the first step, believing in yourself, believing you can do it, and trusting it will work! Keep on growing.

Chapter 14

ABOUT THE AUTHOR

Taking these Diverse Talents: a Bachelor of Sciences in Nutrition and Human Health, Post Graduate Qualifications in Health and Safety, Risk Management, Executive Coaching, and Environmental Management and Sustainability, Rohanne Young has created....

'The Delectable Garden', a company that focuses on the world of healthy and sustainable living, urban environments and growing your own foods!

Rohanne Young is the founder and Director of **The Delectable Garden** and calls herself: Your Personal Edible Garden Consultant.

Tertiary studies in nutrition nurtured her love of growing and cooking her own foods. Followed by post-graduate studies in sustainability and the environment, Rohanne became aware of the positive impact growing our own foods in the urban environment could have, regardless of the amount of space available, whether it be a courtyard, balcony or quarter acre block.

And it all started with discovering a patch of wild asparagus when growing up in a national trust house with an overgrown garden!

From the days of wild asparagus and overgrown gardens, Rohanne has progressed on to creating gardens in diverse climates including the tropics, sub-tropics, temperate and cold zones.

In her life in the corporate world, Rohanne had some extraordinary opportunities: from climbing up lighthouse towers in the Great Barrier Reef Marine Park, to descending into dam walls in the Snowy Mountains and being winched up in a cherry picker, sailing on working vessels and flying through an Antarctic storm to visit Maatsuyker Island, the world's most remote lighthouse. Rohanne is also a qualified diver.

She currently resides in the Redlands, south of Brisbane with her two dogs, three chickens, several fish and lots of garden.

www.ingramcontent.com/pod-product-compliance
Lightning Source LLC
Chambersburg PA
CBHW041427010526
44107CB00045B/1526